Freelancing

Starting a Freelancing Business a Holistic Guide on Finding Freedom

(How to Make Money Freelancing and Build an Entire Career Online)

Michael Hoover

Published By **John Kembrey**

Michael Hoover

Freelancing: Starting a Freelancing Business a Holistic Guide on Finding Freedom (How to Make Money Freelancing and Build an Entire Career Online)

ISBN 978-1-7777356-2-3

Legal & Disclaimer

Table Of Contents

Chapter 1: Finding Your Niche

Identifying your skills and understanding

Identifying your competencies and statistics is an essential step in beginning a a success freelancing profession. As a freelancer, you may need to market yourself and your talents to functionality clients, so it's far important to +have a smooth statistics of what you can provide and what devices you aside from one of a kind freelancers.

Here are a few steps to help you emerge as privy to your abilties and knowledge:

1.   Evaluate your artwork revel in: Take a near have a examine your past work experience, alongside any jobs, internships, or volunteer art work you've got got completed. What talents did you expand in those roles? What did you revel in doing? What sorts of responsibilities or obligations were you especially precise at?

2.	Consider your schooling and schooling: Think approximately any levels, certifications, or education packages you have got got finished. What abilities did you advantage from those programs? Are there any regions in which you have specialized statistics or expertise?

three. Reflect to your hobbies and pastimes: What are you obsessed with outside of labor? Do you have any interests or hobbies that could translate proper into a marketable skills? For instance, in case you enjoy pics, you can offer your services as a agreement photographer.

4.	Look at cutting-edge-day challenge tendencies: Research current assignment trends for your industry or region. Are there any growing capabilities or areas of expertise which is probably in excessive name for? Could you expand these competencies and market your self as an professional in the ones regions?

5.   Ask for remarks: Talk to pals, circle of relatives individuals, or former colleagues to get their thoughts-set in your abilities and strengths. They can be able to offer insights which you hadn't considered.

Once you have got were given got recognized your talents and expertise, you could begin to assemble a portfolio that showcases your paintings and highlights your strengths. This should encompass examples of your past art work, testimonials from clients or colleagues, and descriptions of your talents and records.

The pinnacle paid jobs in freelancing can range counting on the enterprise, location, and get in touch with for for particular competencies. However, proper here are a few freelancing jobs which can be normally taken into consideration immoderate-paying:

1.   Web Development: Web development is a as an opportunity in-call for difficulty, with many companies seeking out to assemble or update their web web sites. Skilled internet builders can command

immoderate fees for their offerings, in particular in the occasion that they focus on famous frameworks and languages which include React, Angular, or Node.Js.

2. Mobile Development: Mobile app development is some exclusive in-call for concern, as many groups looking for to create mobile apps for his or her clients. Experienced cell builders can earn high hourly fees for his or her artwork.

3. Data Science and Analytics: With the growing significance of facts in organisation desire-making, there may be a immoderate call for for facts scientists and analysts. These professionals can earn immoderate hourly prices for their capability to investigate and interpret complicated information devices.

four. Graphic Design: Graphic designers are needed to create trademarks, advertising materials, and one of a kind visual property for corporations. Skilled designers with a sturdy portfolio can command excessive hourly fees.

5.   Copywriting: Copywriters are expert at writing compelling content that engages audiences and drives income. Experienced copywriters can earn immoderate hourly prices for their paintings, particularly if they cope with a specific organisation or niche.

6.   Digital Marketing: Digital advertising is a brilliant problem that consists of seo (seo), pay-in step with-click on (PPC) marketing and advertising and marketing, social media advertising and marketing, and more. Skilled virtual entrepreneurs can earn immoderate hourly charges for their capability to pressure web page traffic and conversions for groups.

7.   Video Production: Video is turning into an increasingly more critical medium for businesses, with many searching out to create promotional films, explainer films, and unique types of video content material cloth. Experienced video manufacturers can command excessive hourly costs for their artwork.

8. Project Management: Project managers are liable for overseeing the making plans, execution, and transport of duties. Skilled mission managers with enjoy in a specific organisation or niche can earn excessive hourly costs for his or her ability to supply tasks on time and internal price range.

It is truely really worth noting that the fees for those freelance jobs can variety extensively counting on vicinity, enjoy, and business enterprise. However, with the proper capabilities and enjoy, freelancers in these fields can command immoderate hourly prices and assemble a fulfillment, high-paying careers.

Remember, as a freelancer, you may need to be bendy and adaptable. You may additionally additionally moreover need to modify your talents and know-how to meet the desires of numerous clients or industries. But via way of beginning with a clean knowledge of your strengths and what you may provide, you may be better placed to discover fulfillment as a freelancer.

Researching the market call for for your abilties

Researching the market name for in your skills is a crucial step in starting a a success freelancing profession. By expertise the choice for in your skills, you may better function yourself in the marketplace, set aggressive fees, and recognize capability customers.

Here are a few steps that will help you research the market name for on your abilities:

1. Look at procedure boards and freelancing structures: Check out system boards along with Indeed, Glassdoor, or LinkedIn, further to freelancing structures like Upwork or Freelancer. Search for jobs or obligations that require your abilities and be aware about what number of project postings there are, what the average expenses are,

and what form of companies are posting those jobs.

2.	Analyze business enterprise inclinations: Keep up with commercial enterprise corporation information and inclinations to understand what abilities are in call for. This must consist of reading corporation blogs or information articles, attending organization conferences or webinars, or following influencers on social media.

3.	Use online equipment: There are several on-line gear available that let you studies marketplace name for to your skills. For example, Google Trends will can help you become aware about the search quantity for unique keywords associated with your competencies, even as LinkedIn's Workforce Report can offer insights into organisation tendencies and machine name for.

4.	Talk to capability clients: Reach out to functionality clients or agency contacts to get a sense of what forms of abilities are in call for. You want to do this through informational interviews or by using way of attending networking occasions.

five. Identify your opposition: Research one-of-a-kind freelancers or businesses that offer comparable services to yours. Look at their costs, portfolio, and advertising and marketing techniques to apprehend how you may differentiate yourself from the competition.

By information the decision for on your skills, you could better function yourself in the marketplace and goal clients which can be most possibly to want your services. This allow you to set aggressive prices and construct a a hit freelancing profession. Keep in mind that name for for precise abilities can alternate over time, so it's miles essential to live updated on agency trends and adapt your abilties and services as desired.

Setting up your Accounts

Creating a profile

Creating a profile on freelancing systems is an essential step in setting up your presence as a freelancer and attracting functionality clients. Here's a greater particular rationalization of what need to be covered to your profile:

1.   Name and image: Use your real name and a professional photo to assemble credibility and consider with functionality clients. A smooth, fantastic headshot is recommended.

2.   Professional headline: Your expert headline have to be a brief, interest-grabbing statement that describes your vicinity of know-how and the services you offer. It have to be centered on what you can do for clients and need to highlight your particular selling proposition.

Chapter 2: Setting Up Your Profile

Your profile is frequently the number one impact that capacity clients could have of you, so it's miles essential to make it as professional and polished as viable. Be tremendous to proofread your profile for errors and typos and use a smooth and concise writing fashion. Including a professional-searching headshot and a portfolio of your quality artwork can help to set up your credibility and appeal to more clients. As you advantage extra revel in and collect superb remarks from clients, make sure to replace your profile to mirror your increase and accomplishments.

1. Name and Photo

When growing a freelancer profile, the name and photo are critical components that could affect how capacity clients apprehend you. Here are a few first rate practices for selecting a name and picture on your freelancer profile:

1.   Use your real name: It's vital to use your actual name in location of a nickname or

pseudonym. This builds credibility and agree with with capability clients.

2.   Choose a expert photo: Your profile picture should be a smooth, notable headshot that offers you as a professional. Avoid the usage of selfies or images with distracting backgrounds.

three. Dress professionally: Dress in a way that is appropriate to your organisation and the sort of paintings you do. If you parent in a innovative location, you may be capable of escape with a greater informal look, but in case you artwork in a more formal enterprise, you ought to dress due to this.

4.   Use a constant image throughout all structures: If you have were given were given profiles on a couple of freelancing structures, use the identical image on they all. This makes it less difficult for ability customers to understand you and allows to set up your personal logo.

5.   Avoid using stock photos: Using stock pictures or general snap shots could make your profile seem a great deal much less actual and can turn off potential clients.

6.   Smile: A fine, approachable smile can help to assemble rapport with capacity customers and lead them to more likely to need to art work with you.

Overall, your call and image must present you as a expert and produce your persona and fashion. They want to be constant throughout all of your on-line profiles and must help to construct take delivery of as actual with and credibility with capacity clients.

2. Professional Headline

A expert headline is an important a part of a freelancer's profile. It is the number one thing that capability clients see after they go to your profile and it must provide them a smooth concept of your abilities and expertise. Here are a few extremely good practices for growing a professional headline for your freelancer profile:

1.   Be clear and concise: Your expert headline should be clear and concise, ideally no extra than 10 phrases. It want to carry what you do and the services you provide in a straightforward way.

2.   Use key terms: Incorporate keywords into your headline which may be relevant in your industry and the sort of artwork you do. This will help functionality customers find you once they look for freelancers with particular competencies or revel in.

3.   Highlight your particular promoting proposition: Your professional headline want to spotlight what gadgets you apart from different freelancers. This could possibly embody your unique information, your stage of revel in, or any specialized skills or device you operate.

4.   Tailor your headline on your goal market: Your expert headline must be tailor-

made to the target marketplace you're targeted on. If you are centered on customers in a particular organization, as an instance, you may need to embody industry-specific key terms in your headline.

five. Avoid using buzzwords or jargon: While it's miles important to use keywords for your headline, you want to keep away from the use of buzzwords or jargon that won't be acquainted to capability clients.

Here are some examples of the manner to jot down down a headline for particular positions:

Content writer: Experienced Content Writer with a focal point on seo and social media advertising.

Graphic style clothier: Creative Graphic Designer with a ardour for branding and visual storytelling.

Web developer: Full-Stack Web Developer that specialize in JavaScript and React.

Social media manager: Social Media Manager with a song record of the use of engagement and growing emblem attention.

Virtual assistant: Skilled Virtual Assistant with expertise in administrative help and assignment management.

In case you need to function multiple specialization they need to be related Data Scientist each of those examples, the headline genuinely conveys what the freelancer does and what their unique abilities and knowledge are. They use keywords and spotlight the freelancer's specific promoting proposition, at the identical time as fending off buzzwords or jargon. By following those extremely good practices, you could create a professional headline that permits to draw functionality customers and installation your non-public emblem.

3. Summary or About segment

The "About" or "Summary" segment of your freelancer profile is an crucial possibility to introduce yourself and your services to potential clients. Here are some great practices to take a look at at the same time as crafting this segment:

1.   Keep it concise: Your summary need to be short and to the aspect, highlighting your key competencies and enjoy in a clean and concise manner.

2.   Use key phrases: Including relevant key terms can assist your profile display up in are looking for outcomes and make it less tough for potential clients to find you.

3.   Focus at the blessings you offer: Instead of surely listing your skills and experience, focus at the benefits you could offer to customers. For example, instead of announcing "I am a web fashion fashion dressmaker," you could say "I create purchaser-high-quality internet web sites that help companies boom conversions."

four.   Highlight your specific rate proposition: What units you aside from exceptional freelancers to your region? Do you have got were given a totally precise skills set or technique? Be first rate to focus on this to your summary.

five.   Use a conversational tone: Your precis want to be written in a conversational tone that feels approachable and quality. Avoid the use of overly technical language or jargon.

6.   Show a few persona: Don't be afraid to inject a little little bit of character into your summary. This will let you stand out and make a reference to capability customers.

7.   Mention some of the past obligations you worked on.

8.   Divide the precis into paragraphs for less difficult reading.

9.   Add your great capabilities as bullet points.

By following these tremendous practices, you can create an effective summary that showcases your capabilities and experience and lets in you stand out to functionality customers.

four. Portfolio

The portfolio phase of your freelancer profile is an critical opportunity to show off your work and provide evidence of your skills and experience. Here are some great practices to examine while growing your portfolio:

1. Include your remarkable art work: Choose your first rate and most relevant artwork to embody in your portfolio. Quality is extra essential than quantity, so simplest include your most effective portions.

2. Provide context: For each piece to your portfolio, offer a quick description of the assignment and your characteristic in it. This permits capacity customers understand the context of your paintings and the manner it pertains to their dreams.

three. Organize your portfolio: Organize your portfolio in a manner that makes experience and is straightforward to navigate. You also can pick out out to group your paintings by way of challenge kind, industry, or skill set.

four. Use visuals: Include exquisite visuals of your paintings, such as screenshots, motion snap shots, or snap shots. This helps capability clients get a enjoy of your layout aesthetic and the great of your work.

5. Provide effects: Whenever viable, consist of measurable consequences or information that show the effect of your paintings. This can assist ability customers understand the fee you may offer.

6. Keep it updated: Regularly replace your portfolio with new and applicable paintings as you whole initiatives. This permits to preserve your profile easy and up to date.

7. If you don't have many paintings samples but, you may upload a few samples from the initiatives you made in publications. And you can additionally add screenshots of your certificates.

8.   Make satisfactory to ask for a client's permission if you want to function the artwork you likely did for him on your portfolio.

five. Rates and availability

Setting your costs and availability in your freelancer profile is an vital part of attracting customers and dealing with your workload. Here are some wonderful practices to examine while placing your prices and availability:

1.   Research business enterprise requirements: Research corporation requirements and costs in your particular skillset and enjoy level. This will help you location fees which are competitive and realistic.

2.   Be apparent: Be obvious about your fees and availability to your profile. Clients admire transparency and honesty, and it allows to manipulate their expectations from the outset.

3.   Consider your revel in degree: If you're definitely starting out, you may want to keep in thoughts placing decrease fees initially to attract customers and build your portfolio. As you benefit experience and reputation, you can grade by grade beautify your costs.

four. Offer package deal gives: Consider presenting package deal deals or bundled offerings to inspire clients to pick out out you over opposition.

five.   Be flexible: Be open to negotiating expenses and phrases with customers, specifically if the mission scope adjustments or if the client has a restrained rate variety.

6.   Update frequently: Regularly replace your prices and availability to mirror changes to your time table or revel in degree.

By following those high-quality practices, you can set costs and availability which may be aggressive, obvious, and bendy, so you can assist you entice and hold customers through the years.

Some Platforms are very aggressive, and you could need initially a low rate and increase it little by little (I started out out out with 5$ and progressed my price 1$ after every successful Job).

6. Top abilties:

The competencies section of your freelancer profile is an vital a part of showcasing your expertise and assisting customers understand what you may provide. Here are a few exceptional practices to observe whilst selecting and highlighting your top competencies:

1. Choose your most powerful abilties: Identify your maximum effective and maximum in-call for abilties and highlight them in your profile. Focus on the abilities which you are maximum professional in and which is probably most relevant to the work you need to do.

2. Be particular: Use unique key phrases and terms that as it should be describe your

capabilities. This will assist clients locate you even as looking for freelancers with specific skillsets.

3.   Update often: Regularly update your competencies segment as your enjoy and statistics grows. This ensures that your profile remains up to date and correctly shows your abilities.

four.   Most structures will permit a confined kind of skills to be delivered with the easy plan so make certain to feature your most pinnacle talents. If you can upload more abilties make certain to feature abilities that could have extraordinary terms and Analysis and Analytics.

five.   These capabilities are import as Most systems has an set of rules that ranks the proposals based mostly on how many capabilities are matched with the hobby necessities.

7. Experience and Education:

When it includes the experience and schooling sections of your freelancer profile, there are a few first-class practices to maintain in mind to help you successfully exhibit your expert history and qualifications:

1.   Focus on applicable revel in: Highlight your maximum relevant artwork enjoy, that specialize in initiatives which can be most similar to the shape of hard work you need to do as a freelancer. Be quality to encompass statistics about your position and responsibilities, in addition to any notable achievements or results.

2.   Use precise metrics: Whenever viable, use particular metrics to demonstrate the impact of your artwork. For instance, if you worked on a venture that led to improved net internet site website site visitors, encompass the share boom you carried out.

three. Highlight transferable skills: Even in case you do not have big experience in a particular company or skillset, highlight transferable abilities which are relevant to the work you want to do as a freelancer. For example, if you have project control revel in, spotlight your ability to control timelines and budgets.

4. Add at the surrender any reports you've got that won't be relative for your headline.

5. Be concise: Keep your descriptions of your revel in and training brief and to the aspect. Avoid jargon and technical terms that might not be familiar to all customers.

6. Show schooling and certifications: Include records about your education and any applicable certifications or training. This can assist show your understanding and qualifications.

7. Provide links: Provide links on your portfolio, LinkedIn profile, or specific applicable internet internet web sites or assets in which clients may have a study greater about your experience and qualifications.

8. Qualifications:

In this detail you can add more records approximately the precise Courses you have got. Mentioning the precept topics of each path and what you have located out.

9. Skill Exams:

Here are a number of the important issue benefits of taking capability checks on freelancing systems:

1. Demonstrate understanding: Skill exams can assist to demonstrate a freelancer's know-how in a selected region, imparting customers with self notion that they've the critical skills to complete a project.

2. Stand out from the opposition: By taking and passing expertise exams, freelancers can differentiate themselves from distinct freelancers on the platform who might not have taken the tests or who won't have done as properly.

3. Increase visibility: Some freelancing systems can also feature freelancers who've taken and accomplished nicely on information tests, increasing their visibility to capability customers.

four. Improve credibility: Skill checks can assist to enhance a freelancer's credibility and recognition on the platform, as customers can see aim proof in their capabilities and understanding.

five. Expand opportunities: Freelancers who perform properly on know-how assessments can be invited to apply for delivered duties or gain preferential treatment from customers.

Overall, taking competencies assessments may be a treasured investment for freelancers in search of to gather their recognition and boom their opportunities for artwork on freelancing structures. By demonstrating their understanding and status out from the competition, freelancers can growth their probabilities of being employed for excellent obligations and building lengthy-time period relationships with clients

10. Identity Verification:

Completing the Identity Verification, additionally known as Know Your Customer (KYC), on freelancing systems is an crucial step for both freelancers and customers. KYC is a way of verifying the identity of a patron, which usually involves submitting private facts and authorities-issued identity to the platform.

Here are a few motives why completing the KYC method is critical:

a. Trust and protection: By finishing the KYC manner, freelancers can establish don't forget with customers and monitor that they may be a legitimate and straightforward professional. Clients are often more likely to lease freelancers who've completed the KYC technique as it lets in to reduce the hazard of fraud and scams.

b. Access to pinnacle charge abilities: Some freelancing structures may additionally moreover offer top rate features which might be simplest available to users who've finished the KYC method. These capabilities can also additionally embody get right of access to to higher-paying obligations, elevated visibility at the platform, and priority beneficial aid.

c. Compliance with guidelines: Freelancing structures are required to conform with severa regulations related to money laundering and fraud prevention. By completing the KYC manner, freelancers can help make certain that the platform stays compliant with the ones guidelines.

d. Avoiding account suspension: Failure to complete the KYC manner can also result in the suspension or termination of a freelancer's account on the platform. This can bring about the shortage of ongoing tasks, evaluations, and ratings.

Chapter 3: Finding and Landing Clients

A purchaser refers to a person, organization, or industrial business enterprise entity that hires and engages the services of a freelancer to satisfy a selected undertaking or challenge. The purchaser is the celebration that seeks the know-how, competencies, and deliverables supplied via the freelancer. They are commonly the ones who initiate the undertaking, define the necessities, and set the expectancies for the favored very last effects.

Clients inside the freelancing international play a crucial function in identifying the scope of hard paintings, timelines, and price variety for a task. They also can have a particular cause or goal in mind and depend upon the freelancer's statistics to attain it. Clients may be human beings, small organizations, startups, or large organizations at some point of diverse industries.

Clients may additionally moreover furthermore method freelancers immediately, via freelancing systems, or via referrals. They are attempting to find for freelancers with the critical competencies, experience, and qualifications to satisfy their venture desires. It is the patron's responsibility to provide clean undertaking requirements, provide comments and path sooner or later of the device, and ultimately have a study the deliverables furnished by using the freelancer.

Successful freelancers prioritize powerful verbal exchange, knowledge purchaser dreams, and turning in fantastic paintings that aligns with the purchaser's expectancies. Building extraordinary relationships with customers can reason repeat industrial corporation, referrals, and a stable recognition in the freelancing network.

Types of the clients:

As a freelancer, you could stumble upon various varieties of clients with one of a kind dreams, picks, and working patterns. Here are some not unusual kinds of clients that you could encounter:

1.   Individual Clients: These are folks that require freelancers for their non-public initiatives. They can be entrepreneurs, small business proprietors, bloggers, authors, or individuals attempting to find innovative or technical help.

2.   Small and Medium-Sized Enterprises (SMEs): SMEs often are looking for freelancers to fulfill precise responsibilities or tasks internal their companies. They may additionally have constrained property or pick out to outsource extraordinary capabilities, inclusive of photo design, content material material material writing, web improvement, or advertising and marketing.

3.   Startups: Startups are newly set up companies with precise desires and rapid-paced environments. Freelancers can provide specialised abilities and expertise to assist startups launch their products or services, increase their branding, or assist with unique responsibilities.

4.   Agencies: Creative or virtual advertising and marketing organizations can also moreover moreover hire freelancers to assist their tasks or control overflow artwork. These organizations act as intermediaries amongst freelancers and clients, offering a ordinary circulate of duties and managing customer relationships.

five. Corporations: Large agencies frequently have in-residence groups, however they will additionally interact freelancers for specific initiatives or specialised skills that are not to be had interior their corporations. Freelancers can provide a clean attitude, specialised statistics, or assist with quick paintings spikes.

6.   Non-Profit Organizations: Non-earnings agencies may additionally additionally moreover require freelancers to help with fundraising campaigns, internet internet web page development, content material material material introduction, occasion making plans, or specific precise duties. Working with non-

profits can offer an possibility to contribute to significant motives.

7. International Clients: With the appearance of technology and far off art work, freelancers have the possibility to paintings with customers from around the sector. International clients can supply various perspectives, precise duties, and probably higher-paying possibilities.

eight. Repeat Clients: Building sturdy relationships with customers can purpose repeat commercial corporation. Clients who've had a pleasant revel in walking with you could come lower again for delivered tasks or suggest you to others. Repeat customers can offer a solid and constant deliver of hard work.

9. Referral Clients: Referral customers are those who come to you primarily based on guidelines from previous clients, colleagues, or your expert network. These customers regularly have a degree of take transport of as

real with and self perception in your skills, making the going for walks dating smoother.

10. Niche or Industry-Specific Clients: Depending to your information, you may entice clients internal a specific region of interest or industry. These clients fee your specialised know-how and facts in their agency-particular goals.

Searching for jobs

After putting the profile and finishing the verifications. You will want to search for relevant jobs, and to get the maximum relevant and appropriate jobs you will need to test some suggestions.

Here are a few extremely good practices for seeking out jobs on freelancing systems:

1. Define your are trying to find standards: Before looking for jobs, define your seek standards primarily based certainly in your talents, experience, and possibilities. This can embody elements consisting of

venture kind, charge range, length, location, and extra.

2.   Use relevant key phrases: Use relevant key terms to your are seeking to narrow down the consequences to jobs which might be most applicable for your skills and enjoy.

three. Sort via relevance: Most freelancing structures provide the potential to kind are looking for for consequences with the aid of the use of relevance, date, or particular factors. Sorting through way of relevance will will let you see the most relevant jobs first, based in your are searching for necessities and talents.

four. Review the project description cautiously: Once you discover a technique which you are inquisitive about, evaluation the method description cautiously to make sure that it aligns together together with your capabilities and enjoy. Look for info such as venture necessities, deliverables, and last dates to decide if the technique is a terrific healthful for you.

5. Check the client's comments and rating: Before using for a interest, check the consumer's comments and score on the platform. This can offer you with an idea of the purchaser's recognition and information of strolling with freelancers.

6. You may also furthermore need to goal access degree jobs at the start as a few Platforms like Upwork classifies jobs based totally mostly on the Experience degree.

Some systems as Freelancer.Com encompass a one of a kind form of Jobs called Contests, Contests on Freelancer.Com are competitions in which customers put up a project short and invite freelancers to put up their entries to complete the challenge. Contests may be a splendid manner for freelancers to exhibit their competencies and win new customers.

Here's how contests art work on Freelancer.Com:

1. A customer posts a challenge brief and devices a prize quantity.

2.   Freelancers publish their entries, that may encompass designs, written content material fabric, or wonderful deliverables.

3.   The purchaser evaluations the entries and selects a winner.

4.   The winner gets the prize amount and is obtainable the task.

Contests can be an exceptional possibility for customers who're seeking out revolutionary answers to a hassle or need to look a choice of different methods to a undertaking. For freelancers, contests may be a manner to illustrate their competencies and gather their portfolio, regardless of the fact that they do not win the prize.

It's vital to look at that contests on Freelancer.Com can be aggressive, with many freelancers filing entries for the equal assignment. To growth your possibilities of triumphing a opposition, it is crucial to carefully check the project brief, observe the guidelines, and positioned up excellent art work that meets the customer's goals.

Contests are first rate desire for logo spanking new Freelancers in particular folks who are afraid of getting a primary horrific evaluation because the entries doesn't depend upon your previous Feedback or preceding Ratings, and in case you the purchaser didn't buy your Entry you can no longer get a lousy assessment.

Pitching your services efficaciously

Pitching your services efficaciously is a critical part of triumphing freelance artwork. It calls that allows you to be strategic, focused, and compelling inside the way you gift yourself and your abilties to functionality customers.

Here are some key elements of an effective pitch:

1.   Personalization: When you pitch your services, it's crucial to show which you apprehend the patron's desires and are offering a solution that is tailor-made to their

specific requirements. This approach taking the time to examine the manner description carefully and customizing your pitch because of this. Use the purchaser's name on your creation and reference particular facts from the project description to demonstrate your records of the undertaking.

2.   Value proposition: Your pitch should simply articulate the price you deliver to the client's project. This way highlighting your strengths, showcasing your revel in and information, and explaining how you could assist the purchaser achieve their goals. Use concrete examples and statistics to illustrate the effect you have had in similar obligations.

3.   Relevance: Your pitch want to be focused on the purchaser's desires and necessities. Don't encompass irrelevant information or frequently occurring statements that could examine to any project. Instead, show how your capabilities and enjoy are without delay applicable to the undertaking available.

four.   Clarity: Your pitch ought to be easy to apprehend and free of jargon or technical phrases that the patron may not be acquainted with. Use clean, concise language and avoid complex sentence structures.

five.   Professionalism: Your pitch ought to show your professionalism and interest to element. Use correct grammar, spelling, and punctuation, and ensure that your pitch is well-prepared and smooth to study. Include a polite and professional remaining that invites the customer to the touch you to talk approximately the task further.

By following the ones extraordinary practices, you can create a pitch that effectively communicates your competencies and understanding, demonstrates your fee proposition, and convinces potential customers to rent you for their initiatives.

Writing a fantastic belief

In case of searching out jobs you can want to ship a terrific thought, as that is one of the most crucial steps in freelancing, because of the fact clients hate whilst freelancers sincerely send a template concept to any approach, they want to recognize which you in fact can treatment their hassle, and that is your chance to show how enjoy you are.

These are a few suggestions to write down a incredible idea:

1.   Read   the   undertaking   description thoroughly.

3.   Start with a 'Hi' and upload the customer's name if viable.

four. Make satisfactory your concept is adapted to the manner description and no longer simply reproduction paste template.

five. Make positive your grammar is accurate so the purchaser can see you are professional. (Use Grammarly extension on your browser)

6.   Write your outstanding abilities that fits the hobby necessities.

7. Write about previous projects which might be like the venture.

eight. Divide your belief into paragraphs for less hard studying.

9. Stop with a closure as ' I am looking earlier to taking walks with you' or a Call to movement as "I am looking ahead to your message to talk approximately all the possible method to this venture."

10. Show your enthusiasm: Let the customer understand which you are enthusiastic about the assignment and interested by jogging with them.

11. Address any troubles: If there are any troubles or capability roadblocks related to the project, cope with them in advance on your thought.

12. Include applicable samples: If you've got any relevant samples of your artwork that showcase your capabilities and facts, make sure to encompass them on your idea.

13.   Offer recommendations: If you have got got got any pointers or thoughts for a manner the task might be improved or optimized, percentage them with the purchaser.

14.   Provide a timeline: Let the customer recognize how prolonged you anticipate the challenge will take and on the equal time as you could deliver the very last product.

15.   Be competitive collectively along with your pricing: Make high first-rate that your pricing is aggressive and steady with corporation requirements.

sixteen.   Follow up: If you do not pay attention lower again from the customer interior some days, observe up with a pleasant message to reiterate your interest inside the venture.

Overall, the important thing to a successful concept is to illustrate your abilties and facts, show your enthusiasm for the challenge, and provide the purchaser with all of the statistics they want to make an informed preference.

Chapter 4: Writing a Winning Freelancing Micro Service

In case of Microservices you can no longer need to search for jobs, but you want to make an appealing and prevailing provide.

Here are some pointers to create a winning freelancing microservice:

1.   Identify a particular need: Focus on a particular need or problem that your target customers have. This could be a specific talent or challenge that they battle with.

2.   Define the scope of the service: Clearly define what the patron can assume from the provider. This includes the precise obligations you will carry out, the anticipated effects, and the timeline for of entirety.

3.   Keep it easy and focused: Your microservices need to be easy and clean to apprehend. Focus on the perfect capabilities and services you provide and avoid overwhelming ability customers with too many facts.

4.   Showcase your information: Highlight your information and enjoy within the location. This can also want to consist of your qualifications, beyond artwork examples, and testimonials from glad customers.

5.   Provide easy pricing: Make effective your pricing is plain and smooth to apprehend. Consider providing one-of-a-kind pricing applications that healthful the wishes of diverse customers.

6.   Offer exquisite customer support: Be responsive, expert, and great while speaking with functionality clients. This can assist construct receive as actual with and a amazing relationship.

7.   Use persuasive language: Use persuasive language to influence capability customers of the charge of your carrier. This may additionally want to encompass highlighting the advantages, showcasing your facts, and using testimonials or case studies.

eight. Optimize your microservice for attempting to find: Use applicable key terms in the understand and description of your microservice to enhance its visibility in searching for results.

Remember that a triumphing microservice isn't pretty much the provider itself, however moreover approximately the way you present it to ability customers. By focusing on the particular goals of your aim customers, showcasing your facts, and supplying terrific customer support, you can create a winning freelancing microservice that attracts brilliant clients.

Closing the deal and negotiating expenses

Closing the deal and negotiating costs with the patron is an important detail of freelancing. It requires powerful conversation capabilities and a easy expertise of the fee of your services. Here are a few recommendations for closing the deal and negotiating costs:

1. Discuss the scope of the task: Before discussing expenses, make certain you have a clean facts of the scope of the undertaking. Ask inquiries to make clear any doubts you may have. And make sure you have were given got all the abilities required for the challenge and you could complete in advance than the cut-off date.

2. Determine your price: Based at the scope of the mission and your talents, decide a price this is low-price and presentations the charge of your offerings. Remember you could trade the price you advised in the concept if the hobby requires more art work than described in the project description.

3. Present your rate: When imparting your rate to the patron, be assured and provide an reason behind the manner it aligns with the price you convey to the assignment. Provide examples of similar projects you have have been given labored on and the effects you achieved.

four. Negotiate if important: If the patron proposes a price decrease than your charge, be organized to barter. Be open to compromise and maintain in thoughts exceptional factors along with the scope of the undertaking, the timeline, and the capability for destiny art work.

five. Set clean terms: Once you have got agreed on a rate, make sure to set easy terms for the assignment. This consists of the scope of difficult work, last dates, milestones, fee terms, how you will speak with the purchaser and what need to you supply whilst the paintings is finished.

6. Be sincere with the purchaser approximately your skills, in case you need to look at some capability offer an reason behind that to the customer and he might also will allow you to try this.

7. Get it in writing: It's critical to have a written settlement that outlines the terms of the undertaking. This can help avoid any

misunderstandings or disputes down the road.

eight. Follow up: After very last the deal, have a look at up with the consumer often to make sure the task is on direction and to cope with any issues or problems that can rise up.

Remember, powerful communication is fundamental to remaining the deal and negotiating charges with customers. Be confident, professional, and apparent at some diploma in the method, and you will be much more likely to steady the task and assemble a a success freelance career.

Communicating with the client

Communicating with the purchaser is a important a part of freelancing. Here are some most important factors to take into account:

1.   Be professional: Keep the tone of your communication expert, polite and respectful. Always use proper grammar and spelling, and

avoid the use of slang or overly informal language.

2.   Respond in a well timed way: Respond to the patron's messages or emails as short as feasible, inside 24 hours on the cutting-edge day. This suggests the patron which you are reliable and interested by the mission.

3.   Be clear and concise: Make high-quality you recognize the purchaser's requirements and ask questions if critical. Provide smooth and concise facts to your verbal exchange, and avoid the use of technical jargon that the customer may not apprehend.

four.   Set practical expectations: Be sensible approximately what you may deliver and while you could supply it. Don't overpromise and underdeliver. If you want extra time or if there are any troubles, speak this to the customer as quick as viable.

5.   Update often: Keep the consumer knowledgeable of your development and

replace them frequently on the repute of the task. This allows construct trust and ensures that the purchaser knows what is going on.

6.   Handle conflicts professionally: If there are any issues or conflicts with the consumer, cope with them professionally and respectfully. Try to find out an answer that works for every events.

7.   If the purchaser desires greater art work than what you agreed to do, ask him to make a today's milestone in case of consistent charge jobs, but In case of hourly price there may be no trouble. But make sure this can not struggle with other jobs you may deliberate to do.

Dealing with tough customers

Dealing with difficult customers can be a hard experience for freelancers, but it is a critical competencies to understand as a manner to maintain a a success freelancing profession. Here are a few suggestions on a manner to cope with hard clients:

1. Keep calm and professional:

Keeping calm and professional is an critical tip while handling hard clients. This method staying diploma-headed and composed, even supposing confronted with tough or hectic conditions. It's essential to preserve a expert demeanor and speak in a polite and respectful manner typically.

When a client is hard, it's far herbal to feel annoyed, protecting, or indignant. However, it's miles crucial no longer to permit these emotions take over and to stay calm and professional in all interactions. This can assist to diffuse nerve-racking conditions and save you them from escalating further.

To keep calm and professional, it can be useful to take a step once more and have a look at the scenario objectively. Try to break up your feelings from the scenario and awareness on finding a solution. Take a deep breath, pause earlier than responding, and select your terms cautiously.

It's moreover important to keep away from getting shielding or taking topics in my opinion. Remember that the client's frustration or anger isn't constantly directed at you for my part, however rather at the scenario or problem handy. Try to be aware of their issues and reply with empathy and data.

2. Be element specific:

Being element-particular can assist in handling tough customers with the beneficial aid of providing clarity and heading off misunderstandings. When speaking with hard clients, it's far vital to be as clear and specific as viable approximately what you can and can't do, what the project involves, and what the client can anticipate from you.

For example, if a difficult patron is requesting a exchange which you can not accommodate, provide an purpose in the back of in element why it is not feasible and provide opportunity answers. Similarly, if a difficult purchaser isn't clear approximately their expectancies or necessities, ask for extra data and provide high-quality motives of ways you may meet their goals.

By being detail-particular, you may showcase your expertise and professionalism, and assist to construct accept as proper with and self belief with the difficult purchaser. It moreover allows you to set clean limitations and expectancies, that may prevent ability problems from arising in the future.

3. Listen carefully:

When coping with hard clients, it is critical to pay interest cautiously to their troubles and courtroom instances. Often, clients may feel annoyed or dissatisfied because of the fact they do now not enjoy heard or understood. By actively paying attention to their issues, you may reveal which you are taking their feedback critically and which you are dedicated to finding an answer that works for everyone.

To concentrate carefully, it's miles important to offer the purchaser your undivided interest. This method keeping off distractions like checking your mobile phone or surfing the internet even as you're speaking to them. It moreover method listening to both their phrases and their tone of voice.

When the customer is talking, keep away from interrupting them and try to make easy any factors which you're uncertain about. You can try this thru asking open-ended questions like "Can you inform me more about that?" or "What specially are you seeking out?" This suggests the client which you are engaged in the communication and which you are running to understand their needs.

4. Be affected person:

Being affected person is an essential talent while dealing with tough customers. Sometimes, customers won't talk their needs effectively or may additionally additionally have unrealistic expectancies, that might reason frustration and strain. It is vital to recall that everybody has their non-public way of talking and processing statistics, and it is able to take time to completely understand their dreams and issues. Rushing the technique or reacting in an impatient manner can worsen the scenario and make it extra tough to discover a selection.

In addition, being affected character can help to assemble accept as proper with and rapport with the patron. By taking the time to pay attention to their problems, apprehend their mindset, and offer considerate responses, you can show your dedication to their challenge and display which you are invested in their success. This can assist to installation a awesome jogging relationship and might reason greater opportunities within the destiny. Overall, while it is able to be hard to stay affected character in the face of tough customers, it is an essential understanding that could gain each you and the client in the long run.

five. Set clean boundaries:

Setting smooth boundaries is an critical detail of handling hard customers. It includes putting in and talking clean expectations about what you can and can not do, what the consumer can assume from you, and what the effects can be if the client crosses those obstacles. The key's to be organisation and everyday in imposing the ones boundaries. Here are a few pointers for putting clean barriers:

Define your scope of exertions: Before beginning any mission, clearly outline the scope of labor and what it consists of. This includes the deliverables, time limits, and any barriers. Communicate this truely to the client and get their agreement in writing. This will assist to avoid any misunderstandings or disagreements later on.

Be clean about verbal exchange channels and availability: Establish how you can communicate with the customer and the manner frequently. Let them apprehend what hours you're available and the way lengthy they are capable of count on to have a look at for a response. This will help to control their expectations and avoid any frustration on both aspect. Make high quality to paste on your verbal exchange plan and respond to their messages indoors an low priced time body.

6. Offer answers:

When dealing with difficult clients, it's far vital to recognition on finding answers to the troubles they are handling. Instead of really affirming problems or saying no to requests, try to provide you with opportunity answers that meet the client's needs even as furthermore aligning with your personal limitations and skills. This requires a aggregate of creativity, trouble-fixing competencies, and a willingness to collaborate.

To provide effective solutions, it's miles important to first apprehend the customer's underlying goals and dreams. Ask inquiries to make clean their troubles and pick out any constraints they'll be handling. Then, brainstorm wonderful options that cope with the ones troubles at the same time as additionally deliberating your personal abilities and boundaries. Be open to attempting new approaches or adapting your regular way of going for walks to higher serve the client's needs. By imparting proactive and innovative solutions, you can display the patron that you are invested of their fulfillment and committed to locating a together useful choice.

7. Know whilst to stroll away:

Knowing when to stroll some distance from a difficult purchaser is an crucial expertise for freelancers. While it may be tempting to live with a patron despite the fact that topics aren't going properly, it's far vital to apprehend while a state of affairs isn't salvageable and it is time to move on. One of the vital aspect signs and symptoms and signs that it could be time to stroll away is that if the patron is constantly disrespectful or unprofessional. If the customer is belittling, insulting, or usually unpleasant to artwork with, it may be time to give up the jogging courting.

Another signal that it may be time to walk away is if the assignment scope or necessities have modified appreciably with out suitable reimbursement or renegotiation. If a consumer is continuously consisting of on new requests or changing the mission dreams without providing extra charge, it can be time to reevaluate the running relationship. It is important to have clean barriers and if you want to talk your expectations and limitations to the patron. If they'll be not capable or unwilling to recognize those obstacles, it may be time to walk away. Walking far from a hard consumer can be hard, however it's far vital to prioritize your very own nicely-being and professional reputation.

8 .Stay on pinnacle of factors :

Always make certain which you are in total control of the scenario. The minute you permit the consumer steer the conversation, you've got were given had been given out of place it. This goes hand in hand with staying calm and amassed. It permits you to steer the communique inside the route you need, otherwise the purchaser getting the pinnacle hand will now not be pretty.

Some customers may be manipulative, and after you permit them to dominate the situation, you would possibly incur losses inside the occasion that they name for refunds, or substitute of merchandise. Staying on top of things guarantees you get to the inspiration purpose of the trouble, and treatment it before it gets out of hand.

9. Keep checking on them:

As an entire lot as you may not need to hold in contact with the difficult patron, it's far inevitable. You want to display how they're doing. Keep track of any transaction you may have with them through ensuring it is going as deliberate.

Chapter 5: Managing Your Finances

Setting fees and pricing your services:

When it includes freelancing, placing prices and pricing your services may be a frightening undertaking. However, it is vital to installation your value and ensure that your profits is sustainable. Here are a few tips for placing prices and pricing your offerings:

1.   Research the marketplace: Start by using the use of studying what distinctive freelancers on your problem are charging. This will offer you with an concept of the going price and help you determine a competitive charge in your services.

2.   Determine your prices: Before putting your fees, it is important to realise your expenses. Calculate your charges, together with overhead charges together with software program program, hardware, and workspace. Also, element in taxes, healthcare, and retirement monetary financial savings.

3. Consider your experience and know-how: Your fees must replicate your enjoy and expertise. If you are clearly starting, your costs will likely be decrease than someone with years of enjoy. However, as you benefit revel in and assemble your portfolio, you could adjust your costs therefore.

4. Remember whilst you really starting on a specific platform without any preceding feedback, you may need first of all a exceptionally low price even if you have a few experience because of the reality you want to have an advantage over the others. You can hold in thoughts this as making an funding in your self and even as you get your first comments you can improve your price.

five. Determine your hourly fee or mission fee: Decide whether or not or now not you need to fee an hourly price or a undertaking price. An hourly price is right for tasks with an uncertain scope or timeline. A undertaking charge is a flat fee for a specific task, and it is high-quality for nicely-defined duties with a clean scope of exertions.

6.   Be bendy: Be open to negotiating your prices with clients. Consider providing discounts for prolonged-term duties or bulk orders. However, constantly make certain that your fees are sustainable and replicate the charge of your services.

In give up, setting fees and pricing your offerings is an crucial a part of coping with your budget as a freelancer. Do your studies, recall your fees, expertise, and revel in, decide your hourly or mission fee, and be flexible in negotiating with customers.

Managing Invoices and Payments

Managing invoices and bills is an critical a part of freelancing. Here are a few recommendations on a way to manipulate your invoices and bills correctly:

1.   Establish clean price phrases: Before beginning any assignment, make certain to installation clean fee terms with the

consumer. This consists of the rate approach, price time table, and any past due rate prices or consequences.

2. Create expert invoices: Create professional invoices that consist of all of the critical information alongside facet your call, commercial commercial enterprise business enterprise name, patron call, charge due date, fee quantity, and price approach. You can use software program equipment like FreshBooks, QuickBooks, or Wave to create expert invoices.

3. Send invoices on time: Send invoices immediately and make certain which you adhere to the price schedule that end up agreed upon with the patron. Make sure to observe up with the client if rate isn't obtained through manner of the due date.

four. In case of Hourly jobs, you will probably use a platform built-in time tracker but a few systems don't have one, so that you may additionally need to apply external tracker as Toggl. But any manner it's miles a superb practice to make a weekly time sheet to offer an purpose for to the consumer the manner you spent the hours and the responsibilities info during these hours.

five.   Keep music of all invoices and bills: It is important to preserve music of all your invoices and bills. This can be executed using a spreadsheet or an accounting software device. This will help you to without problems find out any exceptional payments and make sure that you get hold of price for all completed artwork.

6.   Follow up on past due bills: If a fee is not received by using the usage of manner of the due date, comply with up with the customer to make certain that they are privy to the extraordinary fee. Be professional and polite whilst speakme with the customer, but furthermore assertive in making sure that you acquire rate for the paintings that you have completed.

7.   Consider using fee systems: Payment systems like PayPal, Stripe, Payoneer and

TransferWise need to make it a lot much less difficult to get maintain of bills from clients. These structures provide abilities like regular payments, charge reminders, and automated transfers, that can simplify the charge manner and assist you gets a commission on time.

Tracking your expenses and record taxes

As a freelancer, it's far crucial to preserve song of your fees and file taxes efficiently a good way to keep monetary stability and avoid any criminal issues. Here are some recommendations for managing your budget and filing taxes:

1. Keep music of all of your commercial organization prices: This consists of any fees associated with your work together with device, software utility, workplace location, internet payments, excursion expenses, and more. Make outstanding to keep receipts and invoices for each rate.

2. Separate non-public and enterprise charge range: It's essential to have separate

economic institution money owed and credit score score playing playing cards for your private and enterprise price range. This enables you keep track of your corporation prices and makes it much less complicated to document taxes.

3. Use accounting software program program program: There are numerous accounting software program application applications available, which includes QuickBooks, if you want to will can help you manage your price range greater efficiently. These tools let you song your costs, create invoices, and generate financial critiques.

4. Hire a tax professional: Freelancers have precise tax necessities, so it's crucial to paintings with a tax professional who will let you navigate tax jail hints and ensure you file efficiently. A tax professional can also help you find out deductions and decrease your tax legal responsibility.

five. Set apart cash for taxes: As a freelancer, you are answerable for paying your personal taxes. It's important to set apart a part of your earnings every month for taxes so you're prepared even as tax season arrives.

6.   File taxes on time: Make certain to file your taxes on time to keep away from consequences and interest expenses. The reduce-off date for submitting taxes within the US is generally April 15th, however this could variety relying for your usa or location.

By following the ones recommendations, you may live on pinnacle of your finances and avoid any troubles in terms of taxes and expenses.

Building Your Brand

Building your emblem as a freelancer is about installing region a robust and everyday photo for yourself within the minds of your clients and potential customers. This entails growing a completely unique identification that gadgets you apart from other freelancers and showcases your talents and information. To gather your brand, you should popularity on growing a robust on-line presence through your website and social media profiles, in addition to growing remarkable content material cloth cloth that showcases your abilities and knowledge. You ought to moreover attention on networking and building relationships with customers and unique freelancers in your company, in addition to seeking out opportunities to show off your paintings and statistics through speakme engagements and distinctive events. By constructing a strong logo, you can set up yourself as a relied on and reliable freelancer and attraction to extra customers and opportunities to increase your company.

Creating a non-public brand that aligns collectively collectively along with your place of interest.

Creating a private logo is an vital issue of constructing your freelancing enterprise. Your personal emblem want to mirror your region of interest and the offerings you offer, in addition to your unique strengths and values. To start building your brand, you want to first discover your location of interest and the sort of customers you want to attract. This will assist you create a emblem message that speaks straight away to your goal market.

Once you have got were given got recognized your area of interest, you need to create a logo identity that displays your precise fashion and person. This can include a logo, shade scheme, and typography which is probably consistent sooner or later of all of your marketing and advertising and marketing materials, collectively together with your internet site, enterprise employer playing cards, and social media profiles.

It's additionally crucial to create content fabric that showcases your expertise and demonstrates your value to functionality clients. This can include weblog posts, case research, and terrific forms of content material that provide belief into your company and the services you provide. By usually growing exceptional content material cloth, you may installation your self as a idea chief in your location of hobby and gather remember with functionality customers.

Finally, it is vital to sell your non-public emblem thru severa advertising channels, including social media, electronic mail advertising, and networking sports. By building a strong personal logo, you may differentiate yourself from competition and set up a reputation as a expert and clean freelancer.

Chapter 6: Developing a Strong on Line Presence

Developing a sturdy on-line presence is important for any freelancer who wants to construct their emblem and trap customers. Here are some key steps to help you extend a sturdy online presence:

1.   Create a professional net web page: A professional net website is your on-line storefront and the inspiration of your on-line presence. It wants to reveal off your paintings, services, and phone statistics in a easy and concise way.

2.   Establish a social media presence: Choose social media structures that align at the aspect of your purpose marketplace and vicinity of hobby, and create a sturdy and steady brand in the course of all structures. Regularly publish relevant content material cloth material and interact with your lovers to boom your visibility and credibility.

three. Build a portfolio: A portfolio showcases your incredible artwork and demonstrates your skills and experience. It wants to be smooth to navigate and spotlight your precise rate proposition.

4. Get listed on freelance structures: Joining established freelance structures like Upwork, Freelancer.Com, or Fiverr allow you to get located with the aid of manner of customers who are actively searching out freelancers in your area of interest.

5. Network and collaborate: Building relationships with one-of-a-type freelancers, business enterprise professionals, and potential customers assist you to boom your attain and gain valuable insights and referrals.

By enforcing the ones techniques, you may set up a sturdy on line presence to help you stand proud of the competition and trap extra clients.

Creating a advertising and marketing and marketing and advertising method to sell your services

Creating a advertising and marketing approach is vital to promote your services and attract functionality clients. Here are a few steps to boom a robust advertising and advertising and marketing approach:

1. Identify your purpose marketplace: Before developing a advertising and advertising approach, you need to come to be privy to your target market. Who are they? What are their desires and ache elements? How are you capable of assist resolve their troubles together with your offerings?

2. Create a unique price proposition: You want to have a very particular value proposition that differentiates you out of your competition. It must surely talk the blessings of your services on your target market.

three. Choose your advertising and advertising channels: Based on your goal marketplace and particular price proposition, you need to select the handiest advertising channels to reap them. This can encompass social media systems, email advertising, content cloth advertising and marketing, paid advertising, and so forth.

four. Develop a content fabric method: Content marketing is an powerful way to expose off your statistics and construct your brand. You can create weblog posts, movement photos, social media content material material, case research, and special styles of content material cloth that display your abilties and price.

5. Engage together with your purpose marketplace: It's vital to interact together with your target audience on social media and other systems. Respond to comments and messages, participate in relevant agencies and agencies, and provide useful facts and insights.

6. Measure and adjust: Finally, you want to degree the effectiveness of your marketing and advertising and marketing technique and make modifications as wanted. Use analytics system to song your website traffic, social media engagement, and one in all a kind

metrics to appearance what is operating and what is now not. Then, regulate your method consequently to maximize your consequences.

Managing Your Time and Productivity

Managing some time and productiveness as a freelancer is vital to your success. It consists of setting clean desires, prioritizing obligations, creating a time desk, and casting off distractions. By correctly managing some time, you may growth your productivity, meet closing dates, and preserve a wholesome art work-lifestyles balance. It moreover enables you live centered and organized, allowing you to supply notable artwork in your customers efficaciously.

Setting up a schedule and sticking to it

Setting up a time desk and sticking to it's far critical for dealing with some time and maximizing your productiveness as a freelancer. Here are a few steps to help you set up and preserve a green time table:

1.   Identify   your   first-class   hours: Determine the times of day while you feel maximum focused and energized. This can range from person to character, so become aware about the hours while you could do your tremendous artwork.

2.   Prioritize your responsibilities: Make a listing of all of the duties you need to perform and prioritize them based totally on significance and time limits. This facilitates you allocate a while successfully and make certain that you whole vital responsibilities first.

three. Allocate time blocks: Divide your day into precise time blocks dedicated to wonderful kinds of obligations. For instance, you may have separate blocks for client paintings, advertising, administrative responsibilities, and private breaks. This permits you popularity on unique sports activities activities during each block and avoid multitasking.

four. Use productivity gear: Utilize digital machine or apps collectively with calendars, task control apps as to-do packages as Trello, or undertaking manage equipment as Jira to set up and schedule your duties. Set reminders and time limits to live on direction.

five. Be practical along with a while estimates: Estimate how masses time each venture will take and allocate enough time for every. Be realistic and undergo in mind factors like studies, revisions, and surprising demanding situations. Leave buffer time amongst obligations to account for unexpected times.

6. Minimize distractions: Identify and reduce distractions that could prevent your productiveness, such as social media, e-mail notifications, or noisy environments. Consider using productiveness techniques much like the Pomodoro Technique, in which you determine for a centered length and take brief breaks in among.

7. Monitor and regulate: Regularly observe how well you maintain on collectively along with your time table and discover areas for improvement. Keep song of methods lots time you spend on every task and adjust your agenda for that reason to optimize your productivity.

Remember that even as it's far vital to comply collectively together with your agenda, be flexible enough to house sudden modifications or urgent obligations that might get up. By installing place a agenda and committing to it, you can correctly manage your time, boom your productivity, and obtain your desires as a freelancer.

Delegating responsibilities and outsourcing

Delegating duties and outsourcing is an important problem of handling your workload and optimizing your productiveness as a freelancer. Here's an in depth manual on how to efficaciously delegate obligations and outsource:

1.   Assess your strengths and weaknesses: Identify the duties or areas in that you excel and people in which you may need assist or lack facts. This permits you decide which duties are suitable for delegation or outsourcing.

2.   Define the scope of labor: Clearly define the duties or obligations you need to delegate or outsource. Break them down into specific deliverables and set smooth expectations in terms of high-quality, cut-off dates, and every different requirements.

three. Identify appropriate applicants or service vendors: Seek out freelancers, experts, or organizations who specialize inside the duties you want to delegate or outsource. Look for humans or corporations with relevant enjoy, extremely good reviews or guidelines, and a song record of turning in high-quality art work.

4.   Communicate correctly: Clearly talk your expectancies, requirements, and any essential suggestions or commands to the humans or groups you're delegating or outsourcing to. Provide all the relevant challenge records, get admission to to important sources, and set up a easy channel for ongoing verbal exchange.

5.   Set milestones and checkpoints: Break the delegated or outsourced duties into viable milestones or checkpoints. This permits you to song development, provide comments, and make any essential adjustments alongside the way.

6.   Maintain ordinary communication: Keep an open line of communique with the humans or organizations you have got delegated or outsourced to. Regularly check in on development, address any concerns or questions, and make sure that the paintings is intending in accordance to plot.

7.   Provide comments and steerage: Offer high quality feedback and steerage to the

humans or companies you're working with. This allows them recognize your expectations better and make any important enhancements.

eight. Monitor and evaluate performance: Regularly take a look at out the performance of the delegated or outsourced obligations. Evaluate the best of labor, adherence to closing dates, and standard effectiveness. If wanted, offer greater steering or make changes to make certain the favored effects are finished.

nine. Maintain confidentiality and security: If you are delegating or outsourcing duties that include sensitive information or highbrow assets, ensure that proper confidentiality agreements are in vicinity. Protect your statistics and belongings via jogging with sincere people or groups.

10. Evaluate cost-effectiveness: Consider the economic factor of delegation and outsourcing. Assess the price-gain ratio and decide if it is more fee-powerful to delegate

or outsource certain duties in preference to coping with them yourself. Factor in the terrific of hard work, time saved, and the potential for extra typical overall performance or sales era.

By correctly delegating duties and outsourcing, you could recognition to your center strengths, manage your workload extra successfully, and leverage the information of others to deliver exceptional effects to your clients. It permits you to scale your industrial business enterprise, tackle more initiatives, and keep a healthful paintings-lifestyles balance.

Chapter 7: Cooperate With Different Freelancers

Forming corporations or businesses with unique freelancers may be a strategic method to take on extra complex jobs and offer a broader range of offerings. Here's an intensive manual on a way to shape such organizations:

1.   Identify complementary skills: Look for freelancers who own skills that complement yours and align with the services you need to offer as a difficult and speedy. For instance, in case you're an internet developer, you could need to collaborate with a designer, a copywriter, and a digital marketer to provide entire net website answers.

2.   Establish easy roles and obligations: Clearly outline the roles and responsibilities of every member in the enterprise or business enterprise. This guarantees that everyone knows their obligations, avoids overlaps or gaps in paintings, and continues inexperienced collaboration.

three. Create a shared imaginative and prescient and desires: Discuss and align at the group's vision, assignment, and long-term desires. This shared knowledge will manual choice-making and hold each person stimulated and focused.

4. Define conversation and workflow strategies: Establish effective communique channels and protocols for sharing records, discussing responsibilities, and handling duties. Determine how you may collaborate, share files, and provide feedback to ensure smooth workflow and well timed delivery.

5. Create a prison structure: Consider formalizing your employer or business enterprise through growing a crook structure, along facet a partnership or restrained criminal duty enterprise company (LLC). Consult with criminal specialists to decide the most appropriate form for your scenario and to cope with any contractual agreements or liabilities.

6. Develop a shared portfolio and emblem identity: Create a portfolio that showcases the collective artwork of the group or company. This demonstrates your mixed information and offers capability clients a clean data of the services you offer. Establish a steady logo identification that represents your collective values and fashion.

7. Collaborate on advertising and advertising and marketing and commercial employer development: Work collectively to marketplace your offerings, acquire out to capacity customers, and strong initiatives. Pool your assets and networks to extend your reap and increase the possibilities of attracting massive, greater complex jobs.

eight. Maintain open and obvious communication: Foster a manner of lifestyles of open verbal exchange and transparency inside the business enterprise or employer. Regularly preserve meetings or take a look at-ins to speak approximately improvement, address troubles, and make any important adjustments to beautify collaboration and consumer satisfaction.

9. Establish a honest reimbursement shape: Determine how you could split revenues and allocate profits among corporation contributors. Consider factors along with the level of contribution, understanding, and the complexity of person roles to ensure a honest compensation form.

10. Continuously evaluate and adapt: Regularly check the organization's performance, assessment patron remarks, and discover areas for development. Adapt your techniques, workflows, or business enterprise composition as had to optimize performance, wonderful, and patron pride.

By forming businesses or groups with exceptional freelancers, you can leverage collective skills and property to address greater complex obligations, expand your provider offerings, and increase your ordinary competitiveness in the marketplace.

Avoiding burnout and live endorsed

Avoiding burnout is important for preserving your productivity and average properly-being as a freelancer. Here's an extensive guide on the manner to save you burnout and live stimulated:

1. Prioritize self-care: Make self-care a trouble with the aid of looking after your bodily, intellectual, and emotional well-being. Get enough sleep, consume nutritious food, have interaction in regular exercising, and take breaks inside the course of the day to recharge.

2. Set practical desires: Set possible desires that align together with your skills and workload. Break down larger tasks into smaller, possible obligations to keep away from feeling beaten. Celebrate your accomplishments alongside the manner to stay endorsed.

three. Establish artwork-life barriers: Define clean barriers among your paintings and personal existence. Set precise running hours and avoid overworking. Disconnect from artwork in the course of non-running hours to recharge and interact in sports activities sports that carry you delight.

4. Practice time manage: Effectively manage your time by prioritizing duties, growing schedules, and placing closing dates. Avoid procrastination and stay prepared to reduce pressure and growth productiveness.

5. Vary your artwork recurring: Incorporate variety into your paintings habitual to keep subjects thrilling and save you monotony. Alternate amongst super obligations or duties, strive new techniques or strategies, and discover innovative shops to stay brought about.

6. Seek resource and connection: Engage with exclusive freelancers or professionals to your field for useful resource, networking, and collaboration opportunities. Join on-line organizations or attend business enterprise

occasions to connect to like-minded human beings and percentage reviews.

7.   Find idea and motivation: Surround yourself with sources of concept and motivation. Follow industry influencers, look at books or articles related to your scenario, and are looking for out possibilities for continuous reading and expertise development.

8.   Take regular breaks and vacations: Allow your self to take regular breaks throughout the day to relaxation and recharge. Additionally, plan and take vacations or day off to truely disconnect from paintings and rejuvenate.

9.   Manage pressure efficaciously: Implement strain control techniques at the side of mindfulness, meditation, deep breathing physical video video games, or engaging in pursuits or sports that help you loosen up. Find what works outstanding as a manner to control strain and include it into your routine.

10. Reflect and rethink: Regularly mirror in your art work, accomplishments, and substantial satisfaction. Assess whether or not or now not or now not you're in spite of the truth that aligned together together together with your professional goals and make critical adjustments or adjustments to preserve motivation and avoid burnout.

Remember, it's vital to pay interest for your frame and mind. If you begin feeling beaten, fatigued, or excessively confused, take a step lower back and re-compare your workload and self-care practices. Prioritizing your properly-being will in the long run make a contribution for your lengthy-time period success and entertainment as a freelancer.

Expaning your Freelancing company

Planning for the future of your freelance profession

Planning for the future of your freelance profession consists of setting desires, evaluating your improvement, and making strategic choices to ensure extended-time period success. Here's an in depth explanation of the manner to plan for the future of your freelance career:

1.   Define your prolonged-term dreams: Clearly outline your lengthy-term desires to your freelance career. These need to include financial desires, professional achievements, personal development, or artwork-life balance. Having a clean vision of what you want to advantage will guide your preference-making and assist you live targeted.

2.   Assess your modern-day scenario: Evaluate your modern-day freelance corporation, collectively collectively with your customer base, income, skills, and marketplace developments. Identify your strengths, weaknesses, opportunities, and threats. This assessment will assist you recognize wherein you stand and pick out regions for development or capacity boom.

three. Identify your niche and intention marketplace: Determine your region of hobby or specialised area of understanding inside your employer. Understand the needs and alternatives of your purpose market. This will allow you to position yourself efficaciously, differentiate from competition, and attraction to the right customers.

four. Continuously analyze and upskill: Invest for your expert improvement with the useful resource of the use of staying up to date with organization trends, generation, and first rate practices. Identify areas in which you can beautify your abilties and information. This will assist you to provide more fee to clients, extend your company services, and stay aggressive.

5. Diversify your earnings assets: Consider diversifying your income streams thru the use of exploring new services, products, or markets. This let you mitigate threat and create more profits streams. For instance, you may provide consulting services, create digital products, or discover new industries or client segments.

6. Build a strong community: Cultivate relationships with fellow freelancers, company specialists, and potential customers. Attend networking activities, be a part of online businesses, and actively have interaction in conversations. Building a strong community can bring about collaboration possibilities, referrals, and treasured insights for your freelance profession.

7. Plan for economic balance: Create a economic plan that consists of budgeting, saving, and making an investment. Set aside finances for emergencies and unforeseen conditions. Consider retirement planning and are searching for advice from monetary professionals if favored. Having financial balance will provide a robust basis in your freelance career and provide you with peace of thoughts.

8. Adapt to business enterprise modifications: Stay adaptable and bendy in response to evolving market developments, generation upgrades, and patron wishes.

Embrace new system, systems, or methodologies that can beautify your art work performance and effectiveness. Be inclined to evolve your competencies and offerings to meet the changing desires of your customers.

nine. Evaluate and modify your plans frequently: Regularly evaluate and evaluate your progress toward your goals. Assess the effectiveness of your strategies and make vital adjustments. Stay agile and open to pivoting if needed to align with marketplace desires or private aspirations.

By making plans for the destiny of your freelance career, you could characteristic yourself for persevered increase, success, and prolonged-term fulfillment. Remember that making plans is an ongoing device, and it's miles important to frequently assume yet again and adapt your plans to live applicable and benefit your selected consequences.

Chapter 8: Dealing With Challenges

Handling tough customers

Business isn't, and has in no manner been, for the faint-hearted. Some customers can also reason you enough grief to make you want to drop them, or worse, surrender the business enterprise

To recognize the manner to deal with difficult customers we must first understand what are the kinds of clients and their personalities. Freelancers can come upon quite a few client personalities even as jogging on tremendous tasks. Here are a few not unusual types of clients via the usage of character that a freelancer also can furthermore come across:

1.   The Ideal Client: This type of consumer is a dream to artwork with. They definitely speak their necessities, provide super feedback, and apprehend your information. They understand your paintings and fee your contributions, making the collaboration smooth and a laugh.

2.   The Micromanager: This patron desires to be involved in each step of the assignment and can have a tendency to micromanage. They might also additionally furthermore provide immoderate commands, require not unusual updates, and request more than one revisions. While tough, it is critical to hold open communique and set easy expectations to installation barriers and make sure a successful final outcomes.

three. The Indecisive Client: This customer struggles with choice-making and can change their requirements or route often. They can be unsure approximately their imaginative and prescient or have problem presenting precise comments. As a freelancer, it's far vital to be affected person, provide guidance, and installation smooth strategies to assist them make options efficiently.

four.   The Demanding Client: This patron has high expectations and can be stressful in phrases of awesome, timelines, or scope. They can also push for tight final dates or request additional artwork without adjusting the charge variety. Freelancers dealing with stressful clients need to truly talk their talents, manage expectancies, and set boundaries to maintain a healthful on foot dating.

5.   The Collaborative Client: This customer values collaboration and seeks enter from freelancers as a part of the revolutionary technique. They apprehend your statistics and actively incorporate you in discussions, brainstorming, and desire-making. Collaborative clients provide an possibility to expose off your abilities and make contributions to the undertaking's achievement.

6.   The Difficult Client: This kind of patron also can show off hard behaviors collectively with being impolite, disrespectful, or unresponsive. They may additionally have unrealistic expectations or be overly critical. Freelancers need to live professional, speak assertively, and try and cope with problems or

troubles through open talk. In some instances, it could be essential to re-evaluate the running dating if the troubles persist.

7. The Value-Driven Client: This patron makes a speciality of the fee and effects they assume from the challenge in place of absolutely at the fee. They recognize the know-how and wonderful you deliver to the desk and are inclined to make investments for that reason. Freelancers want to focus on the charge they're capable of supply and align their services with the customer's favored consequences.

8. Clients who do not realize what they want: These customers also can have a vague idea of what they want however battle to articulate their necessities virtually. As a freelancer, it is vital to invite probing questions, offer steerage, and offer guidelines to help them define their goals and undertaking scope.

9. Clients who underestimate your paintings: Some customers may not honestly

admire the rate or complexity of the paintings you provide. They may moreover moreover expect brief and reasonably-priced answers with out information the time, strive, and expertise required. Freelancers ought to educate those clients approximately the price they create and display the benefits of creating an investment in splendid art work.

10.   Clients who ask you to lessen your fee on the final minute: These clients also can attempt to negotiate or good deal for a decrease charge after the mission data were agreed upon. As a freelancer, it's crucial to paste for your pricing shape and talk the price you provide. If vital, you may provide an motive for the reasons for your prices and the scope of the task, however be careful about undervaluing your services.

11.   Clients who nitpick: Some customers may will be predisposed to excessively scrutinize or discover faults for your art work. They may additionally request severa revisions or make useless modifications. It's

vital to set smooth expectations from the beginning, set up revision limits, and make sure open verbal exchange to address their troubles at the same time as maintaining the task's improvement.

12. Clients who disappear: These clients may additionally turn out to be unresponsive or save you speaking in the path of the undertaking. They may not offer properly timed remarks or clarification, inflicting delays and uncertainty. Freelancers want to hold regular communication, set clean deadlines, and set up a protocol for coping with unresponsive clients to mitigate the effect at the undertaking timeline.

thirteen. Clients who're normally on: These clients may also count on immediate responses and feature high desires for your availability. They can also touch you outdoor of agreed-upon strolling hours or require regular updates. It's vital to set up smooth limitations, speak your availability and response instances, and manage their expectancies regarding communique and availability.

14. Clients who do not need to pay: Unfortunately, a few customers may also moreover try and keep away from paying or eliminate payments. It's important to have a clear fee coverage and agreement in area earlier than starting the undertaking. Clearly outline rate terms, milestones, and outcomes for non-price. If troubles arise, communicate assertively and be prepared to increase the problem if essential.

You can cope with even your most tough client in severa strategies, a good way to go away both you and the customer happy.

1. Be element particular: Pay close to interest to the records of the mission and purchaser necessities. Ensure you've got an intensive understanding of their expectancies and deliverables. Being detail-unique permits you to offer correct answers, show your professionalism, and reduce misunderstandings.

2.   Keep checking on them: Maintain everyday conversation with the purchaser to keep them up to date on the improvement of the task. Regular test-ins show your electricity of will and dedication to the mission. It also gives an opportunity to deal with any concerns or issues without delay, retaining off capability conflicts.

three. Empathize even if you do no longer agree: Put yourself within the client's shoes and attempt to understand their mind-set. Even in case you do now not consider their element of view, empathizing demonstrates your willingness to pay interest and find out common floor. It can help diffuse annoying conditions and foster better communication.

four.   Record the entirety: Keep a report of all communications, agreements, and adjustments eventually of the undertaking. This consists of emails, conversations, and any changes to the scope or timeline. Documentation serves as proof in case of disputes or misunderstandings, making sure readability and responsibility.

5.   Be an energetic listener: Practice active listening with the aid of giving your whole interest to the patron's worries or feedback. Avoid interrupting and definitely try to apprehend their goals. Reflecting again their thoughts or summarizing their factors suggests that you price their enter and are actively engaged in locating answers.

6.   Be cautious what you are saying: Choose your terms thoughtfully and avoid responding in a protective or confrontational manner, in spite of the reality that the client turns into difficult or hard. Maintain a expert and respectful tone in all of your communications. Diplomacy and tact can assist de-enhance conflicts and maintain a tremendous working relationship.

7.   Learn to inform at the identical time as it is a difference in personalities: Recognize that conflicts might also moreover stand up due to versions in personalities or taking

walks patterns. It's crucial to live goal and no longer take it individually. Focus on finding not unusual floor and expertise the consumer's possibilities to conform your technique because of this.

8. Set desires: Establish clean goals and goals for the undertaking in collaboration with the customer. Clearly define the deliverables, milestones, and timelines. Setting dreams affords a shared know-how of expectations and allows control client expectancies sooner or later of the mission.

9. Learn the way to permit pass: In some instances, notwithstanding your super efforts, a customer may not be glad or can be excessively stressful. It's crucial to understand even as the running dating turns into unfavourable in your properly-being or productiveness. Sometimes, it's miles better to element techniques amicably and focus on clients who understand your artwork and professionalism.

10. Stay on pinnacle of factors: Maintain manage over the state of affairs by using staying calm, professional, and assertive. Avoid getting drawn into arguments or letting difficult clients disrupt your workflow. Take proactive steps to deal with problems, set limitations, and control expectations. Your professionalism and self belief can effect how the consumer perceives and interacts with you.

By following those recommendations, you may navigate difficult situations with tough customers more successfully. It allows hold professionalism, promotes better communique, and enhances the overall customer-freelancer relationship.

Chapter 9: Managing Undertaking Scope and Closing Dates

Managing venture scope and deadlines is a important hassle of freelancing that guarantees a success mission shipping and purchaser pride. It includes effectively defining the scope of exertions, placing clean goals, and organising practical timelines to carry out the task goals. Here are some key worries for dealing with venture scope and closing dates:

1. Scope Definition: Begin via clearly statistics the undertaking necessities and discussing them with the client. Define the scope of labor, which incorporates deliverables, duties, and any obstacles or exclusions. Document the agreed-upon scope in a assignment thought or settlement to avoid scope creep.

2. Task Breakdown: Break down the mission into plausible duties and subtasks. Assign anticipated periods and dependencies to every challenge. This enables in growing a whole venture plan and timeline.

3. Establish Realistic Deadlines: Set realistic deadlines for every mission based on the scope, complexity, and to be had assets. Consider elements like your personal workload, customer availability for feedback, and functionality out of doors dependencies.

4. Prioritize and Sequencing: Prioritize responsibilities based on their criticality and impact on mission achievement. Determine the logical sequencing of responsibilities, ensuring that dependencies are addressed and that paintings progresses resultseasily.

5. Communication and Expectation Management: Regularly communicate with the customer to manipulate expectancies and maintain them knowledgeable about assignment improvement. Provide updates on milestones, any functionality delays, and any important scope changes. This helps in preserving transparency and dealing with customer satisfaction.

6. Proactive Risk Management: Identify capability risks and annoying situations that

could impact venture scope or deadlines. Create contingency plans to mitigate those risks and cope with any problems right away to restrict their effect on the mission schedule.

7. Time Tracking and Monitoring: Implement a device to song a while spent on every undertaking and display development towards the task plan. This permits in identifying any deviations from the time table early on, bearing in thoughts timely modifications and corrective movements.

eight. Flexibility and Adaptability: Recognize that project scope and deadlines may also furthermore need to be adjusted because of sudden times or consumer requests. Stay flexible and adaptable at the same time as making sure that any scope modifications are well documented, communicated, and agreed upon with the consumer.

By efficiently dealing with venture scope and ultimate dates, you can make certain that tasks are completed inside the defined parameters, keep client pride, and assemble a recognition for delivering first-rate artwork on time.

Coping with periods of low earnings

Coping with intervals of low profits may be a difficult issue of freelancing. However, with right making plans and techniques, it is possible to navigate the ones situations correctly. Here's a proof of a way to address intervals of low income:

1.   Budget and economic planning: Create a sensible price range that reflects your cutting-edge monetary state of affairs and recall your important charges. Evaluate your spending conduct and perceive regions wherein you may cut lower back or store cash. Prioritize vital prices even as minimizing discretionary spending. By having a easy understanding of your financial responsibilities and belongings, you can better manage your fee range for the duration of intervals of low income.

2. Emergency fund: Establish an emergency fund to provide a monetary cushion at some point of lean instances. Save a part of your income on the equal time as agency is proper, and set it aside for emergencies or low-income durations. Having a reserve of charge variety can assist alleviate stress and offer a safety internet whilst you experience fluctuations in earnings.

3. Diversify your profits streams: Explore opportunities to diversify your income through manner of using offering additional services or exploring opportunity assets of sales. This can contain developing your client base, seeking out undertaking-based art work, or exploring passive earnings streams together with on line publications or associate advertising and advertising. Diversification can help mitigate the effect of a slowdown in a single vicinity of your freelance enterprise.

four. Creating profiles on a couple of freelancing structures permits you to diversify your client base and enlarge your gain. Each platform draws precise clients and gives specific possibilities, so thru being present on more than one systems, you increase your possibilities of securing projects despite the fact that business business enterprise is slow on one platform.

five. Seek short-term or issue-time artwork: Consider taking over brief-term or aspect-time paintings to supplement your income at some point of low intervals. This ought to contain freelance gigs, consulting obligations, or perhaps conventional employment. Look for possibilities that align at the side of your competencies and agenda, allowing you to bridge the profits hole till your freelance organisation alternatives up once more.

6. Upskill and put money into professional development: Use durations of low income to put money into your self and decorate your skills. Seek out training programs, publications, or certifications that might increase your statistics and make you extra marketable. Increasing your skillset can

open up new opportunities and doubtlessly lead to higher-paying initiatives inside the destiny.

7. Network and marketplace your self: Stay energetic on your expert community and keep connections with customers, colleagues, and organization contacts. Inform them of your availability and information, and leverage phrase-of-mouth referrals to consistent new duties. Utilize online systems, social media, and professional networking activities to market your services and lure capability customers.

8. Negotiate rate phrases: When stepping into new contracts or tasks, preserve in thoughts negotiating favorable charge terms that provide a few balance in the course of low-income durations. For instance, you can request partial earlier bills or milestone-based virtually payments to ensure a ordinary cash flow. Clear charge agreements and invoices can assist reduce fee delays and make sure

you obtain well timed reimbursement for your artwork.

nine. Stay introduced approximately and extraordinary: It's important to hold a brilliant thoughts-set at some stage in periods of low earnings. Focus on the lengthy-time period desires of your freelance career and remind your self that low-income intervals are brief. Use the downtime to reevaluate and enhance your commercial agency techniques, decorate your talents, and discover new opportunities. Maintaining motivation and a proactive approach will can help you get better more potent.

By imposing the ones techniques, you may better deal with durations of low profits as a freelancer. It's critical to recall that freelancing regularly consists of fluctuations in earnings, and planning in advance and taking proactive measures let you navigate those worrying conditions more efficaciously.

Conclusion and Next Steps

Reflecting on your freelance journey

Embarking on a agreement adventure is like stepping onto a winding path entire of exhilarating highs and sudden twists. As you navigate thru the area of self-employment, you stumble upon a myriad of reviews, challenges, and triumphs that shape your professional boom. Amidst the steady hustle and the ever-changing landscape, it is crucial to pause and replicate in your freelance adventure. Reflecting allows you to get to the lowest of the hidden gem stones of information buried within your research and offers a compass to manual you towards future success. So, take a 2d to stroll down reminiscence lane, have a good time your victories, research out of your missteps, and envision the path earlier. In this section, we delve into the artwork of reflecting on your freelance adventure, uncovering its transformative energy to form your capabilities, mindset, and aspirations. Let's find out the profound insights and valuable commands that lie within the depths of self-meditated photograph as you embark on this introspective adventure of personal and professional boom.

Here's an proof of the significance and technique of reflecting to your freelance journey:

1. Gain self-consciousness: Reflection permits you to advantage a deeper data of your self as a freelancer. It lets in you discover your strengths, weaknesses, and areas for development. By reflecting to your beyond projects, successes, and demanding conditions, you may affirm your abilities, alternatives, and working fashion. This self-interest allows you to make knowledgeable picks and align your freelance career collectively together with your values and desires.

2. Celebrate achievements: Reflecting in your freelance journey permits you to widely known and celebrate your achievements. It's an opportunity to understand the milestones you've got reached, the tasks you have

efficiently finished, and the powerful remarks or testimonials you've got received. Celebrating your successes boosts yourself belief and motivation, reminding you of your abilities and the development you've got made.

3. Learn from mistakes: Reflection permits you've got a take a look at from your errors and setbacks. By analyzing responsibilities that did no longer cross as deliberate or encounters with tough clients, you can identify the elements that contributed to the demanding conditions and locate approaches to prevent or address similar troubles within the destiny. Learning from errors is vital for increase and professional improvement as a freelancer.

four. Identify regions for development: Through reflected picture, you can emerge as aware about regions for improvement and understanding improvement. It may additionally comprise recognizing gaps to your expertise, exploring new gear or technology, or honing your communique or time manage competencies. By pinpointing those areas, you could proactively are looking for for possibilities for gaining knowledge of and growth to beautify your talents as a freelancer.

5.   Set destiny goals: Reflecting on your freelance journey permits you region great and sensible dreams for the future. It permits you to evaluate wherein you need to move, what you want to achieve, and the steps you need to take to get there. By knowledge your strengths, weaknesses, and aspirations, you may set unique, measurable, viable, applicable, and time-sure (SMART) dreams that align in conjunction with your vision on your freelance career.

Chapter 10: Setting Dreams for the Future

Imagine standing on the precipice of opportunity, with a global of opportunities beckoning you ahead. Setting goals for the future is like casting a vibrant tapestry of aspirations and desires, weaving a roadmap that courses you in the direction of your selected vacation spot. It's a risk to channel your electricity, reputation your efforts, and unharness the general pressure of your capability. Whether you envision mountaineering towering peaks of success or charting unexplored territories of innovation, reason putting empowers you to carve a completely unique course for your freelance adventure. With every purpose you vicinity, you ignite a spark of ambition that fuels your strain, propels you forward, and transforms dreams into tangible realities. So, take a jump into the region of opportunities, wherein aspirations take flight, wherein desires evolve into concrete desires, and in which your future as a freelancer becomes a charming adventure looking in advance to its grand unveiling. In this phase, we embark on a quest to solve the art of setting dreams for the future, exploring the transformative power it holds to shape your trajectory, inspire your actions, and redefine the very essence of your freelance career. Let us embark in this thrilling excursion together, in which the boundaries of imagination are boundless, and the tapestry of your destiny awaits its colorful brushstrokes of achievement.

Next steps for developing and enhancing your freelance commercial employer

Congratulations! You've laid a solid foundation in your freelance business employer, however the adventure might now not surrender right right here. It's time to embark at the exhilarating quest of developing and enhancing your freelance empire, achieving new heights of fulfillment and success. As you placed your sights on the horizon of opportunities, a global of possibilities awaits your eager embody. The subsequent steps will check your mettle, challenge your ingenuity, and fuel your insatiable hunger for increase. Get equipped to unharness your innovative prowess, enlarge your network, and harness the strength of innovation.

First, extend your expert network like a weaver connecting threads in a grand tapestry. Attend employer sports, be a part of online agencies, and interact in networking sports that display you to love-minded specialists and capacity clients. Cultivate actual connections, collaborate with fellow freelancers, and capture possibilities for partnership and mutual boom. Remember, your community isn't always actually a web of buddies; it's far a colorful ecosystem of beneficial aid, mentorship, and collaboration.

Second, continuously sharpen your capabilities and evolve like a phoenix growing from the ashes. Stay abreast of corporation tendencies, growing technologies, and new methodologies applicable for your area of hobby. Seek out education programs, on-line guides, and workshops that decorate your understanding and growth your skill set. Embrace the a laugh of learning and versatility, for they are the keys that free up doorways to novel ventures and excessive-price initiatives.

Next, refine your brand identification with the finesse of a grasp artist together with touchy brushstrokes to a masterpiece. Craft a compelling private logo that captures your precise essence and resonates together along side your audience. Develop a fascinating on-line presence via a nicely-designed net website online, attractive content material, and a strong social media presence. Consistently show off your facts, percentage precious insights, and construct be given as real with among functionality clients who're drawn to your brand's authenticity and understanding.

Furthermore, embody innovation and discover new avenues to diversify your income streams. Leverage your understanding to create digital products, release on-line guides, or boom passive earnings streams which incorporates e-books, templates, or software program software answers. Think past the confines of traditional freelancing and permit your entrepreneurial spirit bounce as you loose up new property of sales and extend your impact within the market.

Lastly, in no way underestimate the electricity of non-stop development. Regularly look at your commercial enterprise enterprise strategies, solicit comments from customers, and mirror for your performance. Identify areas for refinement and located into effect strategies to beautify your performance, effectiveness, and consumer delight. Embrace a boom mind-set that flourishes on regular evolution and version.

So, my fellow freelancer, fasten your seatbelt, encompass the winds of exchange, and embark on this exhilarating journey of growth and improvement. Let your entrepreneurial spirit manual you, your passion ignite you, and your dedication strain you to new heights. The avenue may be hard, however the rewards are immeasurable. It's time to encompass the following economic disaster of your freelance odyssey and experience the fun of building a thriving business enterprise that showcases your talents, fuels your ardour, and leaves an indelible mark on the arena.

Chapter 11: Specifying Your Business & Lifestyle Objectives

In order to get began out, permit's talk approximately why you need to artwork for yourself inside the first place. Therefore, I had 3 predominant motives for looking for to art work for myself. The first is that I had a strong interest in advertising and branding. The 2nd is that I had continually yearned for the independence of beginning my private organization. The third is that I have turn out to be honestly useless as soon as I attempted to art work for a person else. My boss drew me aside and said, "Scott, you may in no manner amount to whatever." I can though definitely don't forget that day.

Just making sure you are privy to it So the ones were my goals. I turn out to be superb about the sector I preferred to artwork in. I become conscious that I want the independence to complete my task by myself, loose from interruptions and commands from others. Understanding your actual motivation for being a freelancer is consequently a crucial step in the approach. Consider it in this way. Knowing your holiday spot is critical in case you truly want to make certain that you are shifting within the right path.

First, offer yourself a while to reflect approximately your objectives and the kind of lifestyles you hope to achieve through walking for yourself and being a freelancer. There are some important questions you need to sincerely ask yourself. What sort of employment do you truely want to carry out for a residing, first and vital? Do you need to increase your employer to lease a huge frame of humans or do you opt to hold it small and private? What stimulated you to begin strolling for your self? Are you prepared to assist clients in carrying out their goals and dreams on a every day basis? Which hyperlinks into the question of what form of competencies you currently lack and have to put money into acquiring. These are pleasant a handful of the severa queries you could be asking your self.

But preserve in mind that the primary intention of this workout is to honestly maintain close why you need to artwork for yourself. You need to start considering the sort of freelancer you want to be. Consider searching at a function version or a person you aspire to be like as a way to technique this. All you need are a few crucial subjects to picture. It does now not want to be rather intricate.

Just focus on these three critical elements in case you want to make things as easy as feasible. Like me, you need first of all the useful useful resource of thinking about the sector you want to operate in and the form of rate you want to offer to customers. The second is: What motivates your desire to paintings, and what form of regular autonomy do you desire? And final, how a awesome deal cash do you need to make as a freelancer? Now, if I have been to reply to those questions, I have to offer three unique responses. First, I'd want to paintings in internet format and help businesses in developing landing pages that turn visitors into paying customers.

With a Wi-Fi connection, I want as a manner to paintings from almost everywhere inside the globe. And I choice to make kind of $10,000 a month, it really is a pretty cushty earnings. The reality is that those 3 targets are pretty capacity if you undertake the proper technique, which we're going to teach you. But it's far the cause we're proper here. Right. We need to now discover your object as you currently understand in which you are heading. What devices you aside from the opposition and why customers may additionally want to deal with you especially over all and sundry else offering a similar issuer. And with that, I'll see you within the following bankruptcy wherein we can be finding out greater specifics. There, I'll see you.

Locating Your 'Thing'

What precisely does this advocate and what's your issue? Finding your detail sincerely manner figuring out why human beings would select you, your items, and services over every person else offering a similar issuer. What distinguishes you from others and what makes you specific, then? Every thriving commercial enterprise or logo has one factor in commonplace. What they do. For every pair of shoes you buy from Toms Shoes, for example, the organisation donates a pair to a little one in need. Toms Shoes is just like a tailor that offers dressmaker T-shirts which is probably produced for your actual measurements and requirements.

However, to personal a USB or different object, you do no longer need to be an e-alternate enterprise. Even with out a tangible product, a organisation may also increase a totally particular promoting proposition for themselves. Your item need now not be physical. It may be as sincere as choosing to absolutely artwork with corporations in a positive area or specialization. Coming throughout your issue is as a end end result pretty similar to coming across your specialty.

It is the approach of putting yourself in a function to compete in a roundabout way with the opposition.

There aren't any or only some direct rivals in which you are, so it's miles kind of like you are to your very personal little corner of the ocean. This is frequently known as the blue ocean method. This technique essentially consists of keeping off becoming a few other enterprise corporation that suits into the market as an entire and as a substitute specializing in developing a specialization that sets you apart, which include becoming a internet web page fashion designer.

This might also contain integrating software program that lets in customers to tune client hobby onto a internet site. As a cease quit result, you'll be able to tweak the internet internet website online through the years to make it extra useful for image designers by means of way of considering man or woman behavior. For a social media advertising and advertising consultant, this may entail being able to connect the designs they offer to tremendous employer hobbies and dreams.

This is probably receiving a fee or percent based definitely actually on the consequences you virtually produce for the patron. Clients would possibly adore this because it demonstrates which you are informed about and confident on your abilties as a social media supervisor. The opportunities are in reality endless, but it's vital to come to be privy to your area of hobby and determine out how to present your services or products in a wonderful and welcoming way. Spend some time reflecting on how you can set your self other than distinct freelancers.

Once you do, I can guarantee you that it'll not most effective growth the amount of patron commercial enterprise to procure, but moreover help you draw in the styles of clients you really need to artwork with. And while you discover those customers, you can need to recognize a manner to rate your offerings such that they'll be each appealing to customers and provide the quality earnings margins. And inside the very next session, we can start education it. There, I'll see you.

Chapter 12: Pricing Your Services to Make the Most Money

How an entire lot do your services fee, then? It all is based on a few critical factors, I anticipate. First, recall your diploma of expertise and the charge you can provide in the meanwhile. The 2d thing is the amount of testimonials or samples you can offer to capability clients. The zero.33 element is your degree of self-guarantee and your capacity to marketplace your objects and offerings. Let's wreck down every of them just so we're able to better recognize how you can choose out the prices you need to charge your clients similarly to the fees you may price so that you can flip a cute, healthy income.

The exciting detail is that if you have revel in, you may give fee and have examples of social evidence to illustrate your statistics. Customers who're willing to pay for your capabilities will growth significantly. Let's because of this start with experience. If you've got some years of enjoy running at a format commercial enterprise company, for example, and you want to come to be a settlement style designer, how loads enjoy do you presently have and what shape of price can you're making contributions in your patron? Your skills will likely be as an alternative terrific with the useful resource of this thing.

Therefore, you ought that permits you to charge a honest rate for your time and statistics. On the opportunity hand, if you have minimal format statistics, you can likely want to undercut competition for your vicinity to earn customers and advantage the expertise you want to decorate. Keep in thoughts sooner or later of the Book that you want to be commonly honing your skills. It takes some time and effort and is precisely how I started.

However, the manner of improving your self in a high-quality place is extraordinarily profitable as it facilitates create man or woman and an information of in that you commenced out and the way far you have got long past. I myself started out developing logos for friends and unique folks that truly desired a logo for 3 to five kilos back within the day. At the time, I worked a entire-time procedure, however I simply cherished growing emblems or performing some element I became especially obsessed with.

I commenced out out to develop better and better regularly. I grow to be able to increase my costs as a end result and are attempting to find extra money for my designs. This went on month after month, and I truly stored setting a large a part of the cash I earned again into myself via shopping for books, on-line books, and searching a whole lot of YouTube. I went from charging zero to five kilos for a emblem to charging nearly six hundred kilos for my most clean branding package deal deal in a super deal much less than a yr. My prices have multiplied dramatically on the grounds that then, but this is excellent due to the truth I am able to provide my customers and the groups I deal with more charge. Businesses are organized to pay for that.

Clients are organized to pay for that if you may truly link layout with business organisation wants to assist them gain those targets and desires due to the reality they understand you can assist them get toward wherein they want to be. This is most effective a end result of my paintings being well-represented on my internet site and my abilities gradually improving. Your pay is at once inversely correlated with the price you could contribute. This holds actual irrespective of the agency.

Being sincere with yourself and facts the right price you could provide your clients and the groups you need to paintings with allow you to pick out how masses to fee in your services. The amount of social proof or proof you have to useful resource the artwork you've got carried out up to now needs to be reviewed after you have got a outstanding expertise of methods a whole lot charge you can offer to the marketplace and different channels.

Clients will want evidence that you can offer the results you guarantee and examples of your work. Again, this relies upon for your level of knowledge and what charge you can add. However, as soon as you have got got the revel in and the potential to deliver charge, you need to make certain that you display it in a way that encourages new functionality clients to clearly take delivery of as actual within you and look at you as credible. To do that, ask your customers for testimonials and considered one of a kind varieties of social evidence, together with LinkedIn and Google opinions.

The sincere reason for that is that you need a good way to display to new capability clients that you could satisfy your guarantees. Therefore, demonstrating your capacity to offer the outcomes you guarantee thru proof or social evidence will be essential to securing new business enterprise. Building case studies and blog entries to your website is every other manner to do this; this could seem a chunk later.

However, be honest with yourself approximately in which you're and take into account how you may super present what you do and the price you've got previously supplied to customers. Make tremendous you supply this in a way that is crystal obvious and easy to apprehend. The very last piece of the puzzle is actually selling your items or services; we will cross into more elements in some time about the paintings of selling your offerings. But keep in thoughts that gaining greater clients will depend mostly on your ability for persuasive communication.

In essence, the artwork of promoting includes in no manner in reality promoting something. The conventional type of We have one mouth and ears for a motive Is genuinely quite pertinent to this. Although customers dislike being advertised to, they do want a person who's without a doubt worried within the undertaking, cares approximately their precise desires and necessities, and wants to help them in resolving their troubles. They are seeking out a restore. Therefore, asking human beings to select out you to treatment their issues isn't always your responsibility.

Instead, it's your obligation to pay near interest to what they have to say, summarize it, after which ensure you apprehend all in their troubles actually. Only then must you exercise your know-how and know-how to provide you with a functionality solution that is tailor-made specifically to fulfill their desires. The fact is that in case you nicely finished the earlier phase of coming across your item, advertising and marketing and marketing your provider may be a brilliant deal less complex.

Make a judgment on how a good deal you're possibly going with a view to charge in your services based on how tons revel in you have were given and what kind of social proof you currently have after doing a little studies on what others on your enterprise who do something just like you're charging. The reality is that you could speedy find out in case your pricing is in reality too immoderate or too low; if your fees are too excessive, you may have trouble attracting clients and could want to lessen them.

On the opportunity trouble, you want to possibly increase your pricing and start charging more if you is gaining customers too fast and are having problem preserving up with the workload. As time passes, this can take location. And this is essentially the equal method that I used and hold to apply now. I commonly growth my pricing every three to six months because of the reality I am always improving my capacity set and the fee I can truly offer them. In give up, you'll constantly discover how a brilliant deal you may fee to reach your starting vicinity.

Decide what your place to begin is with the useful resource of taking some time. You also can moreover determine out how a bargain you could rate as a most to earn the most profits thru first estimating how hundreds you could rate in share to what the rest of the market is pricing. Once you've got got a basis from which to paintings, the subsequent step is to in fact increase your purchasers, that is blanketed a chunk later in the ebook. But after that, we will speak about setting up authority and a way to present oneself as a concept chief to your place. I'll capture up with you inside the following chapter.

Chapter 13: How to Build Authority from Zero

If you want to start establishing be given as authentic with and credibility with new potential customers, investing in positioning yourself as an authoritative man or woman to your region is a high-quality float. This could appreciably encourage them and supply them the self warranty to honestly touch you thinking about they'll be assured that you are informed within the trouble. You may furthermore expand authority on your private brand or commercial organization in quite some strategies. The first step, notwithstanding the reality that, is to absolutely pick out the proper conversation technique. Which media works the terrific for you mainly? For example, do you do higher in front of a virtual digital digicam like this or in the the front of a computer composing an editorial? Because, as I'm positive you are already nicely privy to, there's a big distinction amongst recording a bankruptcy and creating a blog submit.

Here, you must play to your strengths and be sincere with yourself about the manner you really communicate and gift your understanding. Think approximately this for some time. Instead of trying to produce numerous severa types of cloth, a number of that allows you to definitely be a good deal better or worse than others, it'll likely be far more powerful to commit it sluggish to producing content inside the medium in that you feel maximum cushty.

I cannot emphasize enough how crucial it's far to prioritize terrific above quantity. Writing weblog entries regarding the world your offerings are positioned in is the maximum well-known approach for setting up authority for your marketplace. This no longer only establishes you as a leader in your enterprise, but in case you positioned them in your net web page or social media web web sites, Google Search clients also can find out you. Concentrate on producing lengthy-form, extraordinary material so that you may additionally additionally write as a bargain as feasible without offending the reader.

The longer someone spends reading your post, the more reliable it seems to Google, and the greater likely it's far that Google will region your content material cloth material higher of their are looking for consequences. Making educational chapters to assist your clients with a particular trouble they may be having and which pertains for your records is each different technique to boom your trustworthiness. An instance is probably a internet internet web page designer writing a economic spoil on a manner to select a excellent area name or possibly in reality speakme approximately the pinnacle website design structures available on-line.

Being confident and as price-targeted as you could at the same time as growing financial ruin content material material is key. Seriously, it's miles that easy. Just make an effort to be as useful as you may and display attention for the viewer's time. Try to pass through all of the filler and bullshit and circulate right to the crucial facts. They want to advantage that. By doing this, you could show to the target market that you charge their time, incomes their self belief in vicinity of losing it.

We all recognize the power of social media, which allows us to percentage lots of terrific visual infographics, carousels, and exceptional extremely good records that may be beneficial to our capability customers. I honestly have a small method in which I create fabric that may be applied on all structures. This lets you generate extra attention with the identical amount of try spent generating the content material itself at the same time as saving you from having to hold in mind each platform one after the other.

Don't overlook approximately to reuse your fabric. You need to now not sense responsible about using the proper same piece of content material in or three months if a exceptional article certainly takes off, allows a variety of people, and receives a ton of feedback. You apprehend for a truth that it generates results and that it's going to create a buzz just like earlier than. Similar to cream, brilliant content cloth material is essential. It continuously reaches the peak. So make sure to make use of it often to make certain that you are making the most of each unmarried asset you produce.

I'll provide a quick tip: I write blog posts and book chapters, however I collect the scripts from the chapters and weblog posts I write. As a result, I'm form of writing the bankruptcy's script concurrently with this weblog submit, it's miles almost like getting obligations finished right away. Simply said, it saves plenty time. Additionally, you need to recognition on two topics even as generating content material fabric. First and crucial, the content material material need to be of the best great.

And secondly, writing or developing it could not have taken you a millennium. Additionally, it wishes to be powerful. However, be careful for being overly inexperienced and dashing topics due to the reality that could decrease the super. And almost approximately content cloth, excellence reigns perfectly suited, I guarantee you. It's usually pleasant to provide one piece of facts that aids 50 individuals in vicinity of hundred quantities of fabric that aid in understanding the general precept. It takes time and staying power to installation oneself as an expert to your subject.

The maximum important element you need to be targeting is making sure that you are everyday and that you are producing beneficial cloth on a ordinary foundation, regardless of the form of content cloth you're presenting, whether or no longer or no longer it's far bankruptcy instructions, podcasts, articles, or Instagram carousels. Spend your effort and time generating material which you regularly percentage with the public. If a patron visits your net web page and finds 50 to a hundred blog entries about the venture they want to hire you for, they may right away understand which you are informed for your place, and the idea and momentum will begin to develop.

This will no longer only assist you lure extra clients, but it'll additionally allow you to charge extra in your time and services. You may be seemed as a expert on your place if you offer notable material related to the organization you provide. Keep in thoughts that your consumer pays for charge. The value that you could offer is what they may be looking for. Therefore, if you may exhibit your capacity and information through the cloth you produce, it'll assist your revenue growth considerably through the years.

The more you perform it all through the subsequent consultation. We ought to speak approximately your portfolio and the pleasant techniques to provide your art work. It's going to be one of the first locations that customers appearance, as you possibly inferred from this financial disaster. Therefore, we ought to ensure that it's far easy and conveys the rate you can provide in a manner this is succinct and simple to recognize. So with out in addition ado, I'll see you at the Book's upcoming consultation. And I can not wait considering the truth that this is surely deciding on up steam. Soon I'll see you.

Building Your Portfolio To Win More Clients

In order to demonstrate which you apprehend what you are speaking about and may in fact establish your authority, you need to provide your art work in a clean and inexperienced way. To gain this successfully, keep in mind some essential hints. And by using adhering to those clean hints, you will be able to set up a immoderate degree of take delivery of as real with with new capability customers that go to your net website online or portfolio page. The first step then is to model your portfolio after the finest for your region through learning from them. So as quickly as I to start with started out out out as a fashion dressmaker, I did this. Being the pinnacle emblem representative within the global became my purpose.

So I located the area's top planning corporations and noticed how they offered their art work to capability customers in addition to how they led them thru the responsibilities that they had finished for past clients and groups. The employer's capability to illustrate its strategic wondering modified into one of the key differences. The international's extra traditional businesses all recognized the want of outlining their method and how they arrived on the supposed outcome.

Therefore, demonstrating no longer actually the consequences however also the way you arrived at them will really assist you establish that degree of self assurance and take delivery of as real with with feasible new clients who want to look now not most effective what you probably did for the consumer but additionally the manner you arrived at that unique scenario. Spend a while locating the pinnacle groups or provider providers for your location or region. Find out why they'll be so adept at selling their art work on web sites, social media, and in any other setting wherein you can view it further to their portfolio.

This will offer you a head start and assist you in building a entire and thrilling portfolio that will help you lure new customers and companies. Another top notch piece of advice is to interest at the forestall final effects. As previously stated, your customers are seeking out a method to their issues, now not only a carrier company. It may be very vital to undergo this in mind. The wishes of a patron searching for to lease a internet site fashion designer bypass past easy internet web page introduction. They want a completely last internet web site this is tailor-made to their unique needs and business organization goals.

When new ability customers look at your artwork, it is critical that you take them on a experience. You need to hold in thoughts that the number one purpose of having a portfolio is to suggest to capacity clients that you can provide the outcomes they want. Consequently, endure this in mind while you start to develop your portfolio. You should possibly now be asking how, due to the fact you're basically beginning from scratch, you could prepare a portfolio and show your paintings.So, if this is the case, please do no longer be alarmed. This might be included in a future monetary catastrophe. Keep reading, and I'll see you within the following bankruptcy.

Chapter 14: How to Create a Strong

Therefore, growing your non-public emblem is simply quite corresponding to growing your portfolio's authority. The exquisite issue is that you can use a person who's already successful in your discipline or region as a model for a manner to create a strong private emblem. The first step in growing a non-public brand is to apprehend that it takes time. It does not stand up all at once or in a unmarried day. The pronouncing "it takes many years to assemble a popularity and approximately 5 mins to break it" is attributed to Warren Buffett.

Additionally, a brand is essentially most effective a popularity. Therefore, proper proper here, reputation-constructing is essential. But how precisely are you able to set up a popularity? Actually, popularity constructing follows a fairly honest formulation: provide charge, upload credibility and receive as genuine with, and multiply over time. So that we are able to absolutely realise each element, allow's dissect this. The diploma to which the individual has benefited from information you is referred to as price introduced. This can also come thru reading about a challenge in your portfolio and discovering the manner you really met a client's wishes.

Another option is a honest weblog article that the purchaser might likely employ to get over a hassle they may be currently having. Your diploma of professionalism, self-presentation, and logo credibility all make contributions to your diploma of recall and credibility. How expert-searching is your profile image? Do you, for instance, answer inquiries from capacity clients really and concisely? Do you have got a whole lot of testimonials from respectable clients that you've served? Can you offer proof of the wonderful consequences you have had to your location? The rate furnished can reason credibility and accept as true with. To be sincere, they form of supplement every different.

And remaining, time. Once you have started out the system of growing receive as actual with and credibility by supplying rate, imparting oneself professionally, and accumulating social proof, all it without a doubt is left is time. As your reputation builds, it takes time for others to take a look at you and are to be had to remember you. It might not be feasible to installation a reputation right away. It's vital to method it as a marathon in place of a sprint, as I actually have said.Please take the time, give attention to imparting price, and accumulate as a remarkable deal social proof as you can to installation consider and reputation. Doing so will help you earn new employer again and again in the destiny.

Building A Successful Clientele From Scratch

So, you might be asking how you may show your portfolio if you do not really have any paying customers to begin with. That's all there may be to it. At least no longer the ones paying hefty prices; you do now not want paying customers at to start with. Let me percentage with you a piece tale. I used to collaborate with special humans on their branding after I to start with started out out developing trademarks. I did not price some aspect near what the industrial organization agency is currently charging. The reality is that I wasn't almost as informed and couldn't provide nearly as loads cost as I do now.

Therefore, the fact that I could not provide as a exceptional deal price in my designs have become successfully contemplated in my expenses, that have been moreover no longer very super. However, as time passed and I collected greater data and know-how, the first-rate of the artwork I can also need to deliver and supply drastically advanced. I became capable of fee more for my offerings for this reason, and I additionally attracted clients who've been extra hooked up and consequently had smaller budgets. What then is the bankruptcy on this? So, is it possible to boom a customers with none preceding revel in? You can, truly.

But you'll want to get knowledgeable, get revel in, and learn how to be gifted at the carrier you need to provide through reading, reading, and practising. Like I did, you could ought to start off via strolling for subsequent to now not a few element or even for no longer some thing for you to set up a clients and show your properly nicely well worth within the place you need to art work in.

If you're a website fashion clothier, you could get maintain of a share of the general earnings from the classified ads you have designed in case you had been coping with Facebook advertising and advertising and marketing for a consumer. Additionally, you may get maintain of a element of each lead that is produced through the usage of the net internet site on line you created. So getting a client is the primary stage in growing your shoppers. It does no longer take a look at which you want to be compensated for it, but it might be correct.

The truth is that till you can display your competence, no character can have any reason to accept as genuine with you. Therefore, if you lack any expertise, be prepared to begin going for walks with others right away for a reduced fee or even for nothing. Until you are honestly expert at what you want to be doing, this is excellent a manner to get your foot in the door. If you observe this approach, I can assure you that you may building up enough momentum to in the long run start charging a truthful charge in your products and it sluggish.

Literally, all you need to do to growth the dimensions of your clients is to gain enjoy, progressively installation a solid popularity, and effectively market your activity, as we referred to in the previous chapter. Let's have a look at a manner to acquire social proof and a manner to effectively display it in your net website online and wonderful property. And with that, I'll see you at the subsequent meeting.

In order to illustrate which you recognize what you're speaking about and may honestly installation your authority, you want to provide your artwork in a clear and inexperienced way. To collect this efficiently, keep in mind some essential recommendations. And through adhering to these easy suggestions, you'll be able to installation a excessive degree of believe with new functionality clients that go to your internet net web page or portfolio page. The first step then is to model your portfolio after the finest in your location with the useful resource of analyzing from them. So after I to begin with commenced out as a style dressmaker, I did this. Being the pinnacle emblem representative in the global changed into my intention.

So I decided the vicinity's pinnacle making plans corporations and noticed how they furnished their art work to functionality customers in addition to how they led them thru the initiatives that they had completed for past clients and groups. The company's capability to illustrate its strategic thinking emerge as one of the key variations. The global's greater ordinary agencies all identified the need of outlining their approach and the manner they arrived on the supposed final consequences.

Therefore, demonstrating not truly the consequences however additionally how you arrived at them will absolutely assist you set up that degree of self perception and acquire as proper with with viable new clients who want to peer not best what you probable did for the consumer however furthermore the way you arrived at that particular condition. Spend some time finding the top corporations or issuer vendors in your region or region. Find out why they will be so adept at promoting their work on web sites, social media, and in every different installing which you may view it similarly to their portfolio.

This will provide you a head begin and assist you in building an entire and thrilling portfolio to help you trap new customers and groups. Another splendid piece of recommendation is to consciousness on the end very last outcomes. As formerly said, your customers are looking for a technique to their troubles, now not only a company provider. It can be very important to go through this in mind. The desires of a customer looking for to rent a net web site clothier move beyond simple net website introduction. They need a completely ultimate internet website on line that is tailor-made to their unique demands and commercial enterprise dreams.

When new capability clients check your artwork, it's miles essential which you take them on a ride. You ought to hold in mind that the main motive of having a portfolio is to illustrate to ability clients that you could provide the consequences they need. Consequently, go through this in thoughts while you begin to expand your portfolio. You might also now be asking how, because you're essentially beginning from scratch, you could put together a portfolio and show your art work.So, if it clearly is the case, please do no longer be alarmed. This might be covered in a destiny financial disaster. Keep reading, and I'll see you inside the following bankruptcy.

How to Create A Strong Personal Brand

Therefore, developing your personal logo is truely quite just like developing your portfolio's authority. The incredible element is that you may use someone who's already a success on your discipline or sector as a version for a manner to create a strong personal emblem. The first step in developing a personal brand is to recognize that it takes time. It does now not rise up or in a single day. The pronouncing "it takes two decades to construct a recognition and about 5 mins to break it" is attributed to Warren Buffett.

Additionally, a logo is basically simplest a recognition. Therefore, right right here, recognition-building is vital. But how exactly are you capable of set up a reputation? Actually, recognition building follows a reasonably honest components: deliver price, upload credibility and agree with, and multiply over time. So that we are capable of definitely understand each factor, let's dissect this. The degree to which the character has benefited from information you is referred to as charge delivered. This may also moreover

moreover come via studying about a undertaking in your portfolio and coming across the manner you certainly met a purchaser's desires.

Another alternative is a truthful blog article that the client may also employ to get over a trouble they're currently having. Your degree of professionalism, self-presentation, and emblem credibility all make a contribution to your degree of accept as real with and credibility. How expert-looking is your profile photograph? Do you, for example, answer inquiries from functionality clients virtually and concisely? Do you have quite a few testimonials from respectable clients that you've served? Can you offer proof of the great consequences you have got had to your area? The charge supplied can motive credibility and trust. To be honest, they form of complement one another.

And last, time. Once you have got began out out the approach of growing take delivery of as true with and credibility thru offering rate, imparting oneself professionally, and collecting social evidence, all it is left is time. As your reputation builds, it takes time for others to discover approximately you and are to be had to keep in thoughts you. It might not be viable to establish a recognition proper now. It's vital to approach it as a marathon in vicinity of a dash, as I actually have said.Please take some time, interest on offering price, and acquire as thousands social proof as you could to set up receive as real with and popularity. Doing so will assist you earn new commercial enterprise time and again inside the future.

Chapter 15: Building a Successful Clientele from Scratch

So, you is probably asking how you could display your portfolio if you don't honestly have any paying clients to begin with. That's all there may be to it. At least no longer the ones paying hefty costs; you do not want paying customers at first of all. Let me percentage with you a bit story. I used to collaborate with different people on their branding after I first of all started out developing emblems. I failed to rate a few factor close to what the employer organisation is currently charging. The truth is that I wasn't almost as informed and couldn't provide almost as thousands price as I do now.

Therefore, the reality that I could not offer as a top notch deal charge in my designs became correctly contemplated in my costs, which have been moreover not very exquisite. However, as time exceeded and I accrued more knowledge and knowledge, the exceptional of the art work I can also want to provide and deliver drastically advanced. I grow to be capable of charge greater for my offerings accordingly, and I additionally attracted clients who've been extra hooked up and consequently had smaller budgets. What then is the chapter in this? So, is it viable to expand a customers with none previous enjoy? You can, actually.

But you will need to get knowledgeable, get revel in, and discover ways to be proficient at the service you want to offer by way of the usage of reading, reading, and schooling. Like I did, you will possibly want to start out with the useful useful resource of working for next to nothing or maybe for no longer some thing so you can set up a customers and show off your nicely nicely well worth within the location you want to artwork in.

If you're a website clothier, you can accumulate a share of the overall sales from the commercials you have got designed in case you have been dealing with Facebook advertising for a customer. Additionally, you may get maintain of a portion of every lead this is produced thru the internet site you created. So getting a client is the first level in growing your shoppers. It does no longer comply with which you need to be compensated for it, but it'd be specific.

The truth is that until you may display your competence, no one may have any reason to believe you. Therefore, if you lack any facts, be organized to begin running with others proper away for a reduced rate or perhaps for not anything. Until you are virtually professional at what you need to be doing, this is best a manner to get your foot within the door. If you study this approach, I can guarantee you that you'll constructing up enough momentum to ultimately start charging a sincere charge on your merchandise and some time.

Literally, all you need to do to growth the size of your customers is to benefit experience, step by step establish a strong recognition, and effectively market your hobby, as we cited within the previous financial ruin. Let's have a examine a way to benefit social proof and a manner to efficiently show it for your website and precise belongings. And with that, I'll see you at the subsequent meeting.

Gathering Different Types of Social Proof

One of the greatest techniques to set up your reputation and receive as actual with in any unique industrial business enterprise is thru social evidence. There are numerous techniques for growing social proof. But first, permit's define social proof in its truest experience. Therefore, social evidence is a intellectual and sociological phenomena wherein people try and undertake conduct in any given scenario by imitating the behavior of others. In one of a kind terms, it definitely presents humans with the self guarantee that they may be making the proper choice whilst considering running with you.

Social evidence can take many precise forms. The first is professional social evidence, that is a professional to your field endorsing your gadgets or services and being linked for your emblem. An example of this will be a social media shout-out from a professional on your particular subject. A superstar helping your gadgets or offerings is in reality your way of proving which you are an expert to your field.

Once more, this will be a tweet from a well-known person or an influencer who is largely confirming your authenticity. The next step is customer social proof, in which your gift clients essentially endorse your devices and offerings based totally totally on their interactions alongside side your business enterprise. An example can be taken into consideration one in each of your customers praising you on social media. The understanding of the multitude comes next. This type of social evidence takes area on the same time as a massive amount of human beings appear to be endorsing your emblem, as in the case of getting tens of hundreds of thousands of customers or a massive following on social media.

Validating knowledge is available in 5th. When you deliver understanding or data, a piece of content cloth or maybe a submit receives a commendable diploma of reputation from a respectable variety of humans, that is what you're doing. The 6th object is certification. When you obtain a seal of approval from a key player in your sector, together with the blue checkmark on Twitter or Facebook, you are displaying this form of social evidence. This may additionally entail retaining a college diploma, a master's degree, or a doctorate. As you could see, there are a whole lot of strategies to get social evidence as you try and increase your emblem and business enterprise.

But ensuring you ask for social proof is one of the most underappreciated and smooth strategies to reap it. A smart approach to encourage customers to do this is to request some shape of social proof shortly in advance than turning in the undertaking's very last additives. For example, in case you are assembling the final files for a purchaser, you may likely truely upload which you'd surely find it impossible to resist in the event that they left you some shape of evaluate right now in advance than turning inside the final files—possibly on LinkedIn or Facebook.

Just renowned that it'll enable you to fulfill greater high-quality purchasers who are similar to them. This may additionally in all likelihood lead them to take delivery of as real with that they will get maintain of the ones elements an entire lot extra fast in the event that they offer you with a evaluation. Whether or now not that is the case, you can gain appreciably shifting in advance if it enables you to growth the quantity of opinions and likes on Facebook, LinkedIn, and Google. Each and every evaluation gives up and offers your industrial organisation greater agree with and authority. So hold to accumulate them usually over the years and be given as true with in the technique.

Don't be hesitant to ask customers for comments on their enjoy jogging with you and whether or not or now not or no longer they may be glad with the charge you provide to them. If they may be pleased with the company you have got furnished, there is no cause why they could not spend a few minutes writing a fairly sincere evaluation for you. In the worst scenario, they may precise dissatisfaction with the carrier you gave or provide you recommendations for a manner to enhance it for the following customer.

You also can even create a free virtual asset to offer away as a present to clients who do take the time to head away you a high satisfactory evaluate if you really need to get modern with producing social proof. Now, this may be considered as immoral or even as bribery, however it's miles the objective. You also can utilize the identical object again to assist inspire customers to publish reviews with the aid of way of creating an funding in its development and devoting hours to its creation. You may additionally even offer it out to clients who are inquisitive about jogging with you to illustrate your know-how.

Always recall to assume creatively. The impact of social evidence is extensive, and it best grows more potent as you create and gather extra of it. Consequently, keep this in mind. The fee of aiming to be the fine in the global in your craft may be discussed in more element within the next monetary ruin. So, I want you're organized because of the reality this financial disaster will astound you. In the very next financial damage, I'll meet you.

Chapter 16: The Value of Pursuing Excellence

A winner takes the entire international, writes Seth Gordon in his e-book The Dip States that we stay in. That definitely method that during case you are the great in the global at a few aspect, humans will respect you greater, you may be capable of earn hundreds extra cash, and you could moreover be presented with masses higher possibilities. As an instance handiest. The pinnacle tennis participant within the global, Roger Federer, earned 106.Three% of one thousand million greenbacks in 2020. The 2d-satisfactory participant, Djokovic, made only $forty 4 million at a few level in the identical year. I recommend.

A $40 four million fee variety stays a giant sum of money. But you be aware wherein I'm going. The notable individual at whatever is commonly the only that everybody wants to paintings with or aspires to be like, therefore this equal precept holds right in each place. One issue pertains to the preceding monetary spoil's dialogue about coming across your component on the seashore. The secret is to narrow your consciousness rather than initially searching for to be overly large.

So permit me ask you a query. Is it viable to grow to be the pleasant net site builder inside the global? Yes, it's far, but it'll take you a totally, very, very, very long term to get there—possibly even a decade or . Would it is viable so you can try and be the best within the worldwide at developing logos for non-public manufacturers or probably the outstanding within the global at developing web sites for dentists? Can you spot how, for instance, honing in and becoming the notable at some thing a touch extra location of hobby can not best make your functionality to grow to be the satisfactory in that specific subject a extremely good deal greater attainable, however it is able to moreover deliver capacity customers looking for a gap carrier and a tremendous cause to pick out you and pay you more in your offerings over others who they most possibly see as extra of a commodity.

So, if you want to move decrease lower lower back and polish what you're doing to be the pinnacle in a given enterprise, do it proper now. Or when you have no longer quite made up your thoughts about what you need to perform, now may be the great possibility to accomplish that. Don't strain too much approximately deciding on incorrectly at this factor. To be absolutely honest with you, there can be no proper or wrong preference so long as you awareness on a topic which you are simply obsessed with; it's miles honestly imagined to get you shifting inside the right course.

Later on, you may without issues switch to a few component high-quality. It's vital to realize purchaser management competencies so you may also additionally furthermore get the quality outcome viable with your clients after you have got were given a solid customers base, a high-quality portfolio, enjoy outdoor of a fantastic organisation, pick out out your element, and in reality start operating with customers. And in case you failed to already wager, we are going to be delving more into it within the very next bankruptcy. I'll see you rapidly.

How to Manage Customers and Promote Loyalty

With the exception of that one time they received a unfastened bucket of popcorn at the movie theater, this is always going to be hard to top, you have got your first client organized to provide them the great provider they have got ever acquired in their lives. But joking aside, how do you manage clients and, extra crucially, their expectancies that allows you to help them in following your approach and making sure that they are without a doubt thrilled at the realization of it? In order to make sure that each customer you figure with feels desired thru you as a purchaser and is stimulated to employ your offerings over and over, there are some crucial suggestions to observe.

The first is to be thorough for your wondering before starting art work at the side of your consumer. Asking masses of questions will assist you to thoroughly understand the task and make sure which you are aware about the precise expectancies the customer has in your collaboration. Knowing precisely what the consumer desires to accomplish while walking with you can assist you to recognize the right very last outcomes they're searching for.

Then, you can create an answer that meets those precise desires and specs. You may additionally decide to address any patron who expresses interest in operating with you, however make sure to hold an eye fixed fixed out for individuals who will purpose you some hassle along the way. These are generally the customers which is probably unsure about their desires. As a cease end result, they assume searching at a large array of variations of your art work to soothe their worry or clients who start trying charge negotiations as soon as they start jogging with you. These are normally large crimson flags within the global of issuer, imparting, and freelancing because of the reality they normally propose that the customer is greater interested in getting a bargain and losing some time than they will be in getting the super cease end result and in fact working to advantage that end result.

A piece of recommendation. If a consumer acts in this way, with politeness refuse the provide and preserve taking walks. You do now not want to tackle every customer that knocks on your door the following time; actually plan earlier, anticipate the deadlines, and cling to them. Clients will want to understand even as their task might be added, so pay hobby. They want to apprehend while some thing will arrive in their electronic mail an amazing manner to live up for it.

In truth, it is essential that you spend the time explaining in your client how lengthy the approach will take. This is simplest to make sure which you are on the equal net net page from the start. It's important to hold your client's trust at some point of the process thinking about that as quickly as it's out of place, it may be quite difficult to regain it. Keep your patron knowledgeable, then.